FOR GIVE NESS

A Path to Create Miracles

JANIA AEBI

FOR
GIVE
NESS

A Path to Create Miracles

FORGIVENESS
A Path to Create Miracles

Copyright © 2020 Jania Aebi

The views expressed by the author in reference to specific people in this book represent entirely their own individual opinions and are not in any way reflective of the views of Capucia, LLC. We assume no responsibility for errors, omissions, or contradictory interpretations of the subject matter herein.

Capucia, LLC does not warrant the performance, effectiveness, or applicability of any websites listed in or linked to this publication. The purchaser or reader of this publication assumes responsibility for the use of these materials and information. Capucia, LLC shall in no event be held liable to any party for any direct, indirect, punitive, special, incidental, or any other consequential damages arising directly or indirectly from any use of this material. Techniques and processes given in this book are not to be used in place of medical or other professional advice.

No part of this book may be reproduced or transmitted in any form, or by any means, electronic or mechanical, including photography, recording, or in any information storage or retrieval system, without written permission from the author or publisher, except in the case of brief quotations embodied in articles and reviews.

The material in this book is provided for informational purposes only. It should not be used as a substitute for professional medical advice, diagnosis or treatment. It is the reader's responsibility to research the completeness and usefulness of opinions, services and other information found in this book. Readers are responsible for their own actions. Some names have been changed to protect the privacy of some individuals.

Published by:
Capucia, LLC
211 Pauline Drive #513
York, PA 17402
www.capuciapublishing.com

ISBN: 978-1-945252-83-9
Library of Congress Control Number: 2020911803

Cover Design: Ranilo Cabo
Layout: Ranilo Cabo
Editor and Proofreader: Janis Hunt Johnson (Ask Janis LLC)
Book Midwife: Carrie Jareed

Printed in the United States of America

CONTENTS

Introduction: Forgiveness Is the Missing Link to Success   1

PART 1: The Many Facets of Forgiveness   **13**
Chapter 1: What Forgiveness Is and What It Isn't   15
Chapter 2: Why We Resist Forgiveness   39
Chapter 3: Why Forgiveness Works and Why It Doesn't   55
Chapter 4: The Five Signs of a Need to Forgive   79
Chapter 5: Who and What to Forgive   93
Chapter 6: The Four Levels of Forgiveness   109

PART 2: The Ascension Path of Forgiveness   **121**
Chapter 7: Level 1—Forgiveness as Victim   123
Chapter 8: Level 2—Forgiveness as Creator   143
Chapter 9: Level 3—Forgiveness as Channel   155
Chapter 10: Level 4—Forgiveness from Oneness   175
Chapter 11: Radical Forgiveness that Heals the World   189
Chapter 12: Conclusion—Forgiveness as a Way of Life   203

Appendix—Additional Exercises   215
About The Author   221
Acknowledgments   223
Bibliography   225

INTRODUCTION

FORGIVENESS IS THE MISSING LINK TO SUCCESS

Forgiveness is the most powerful practice for creating the life of your dreams. You've probably never thought of it quite like that, but if it's true, wouldn't you want to learn about it? You probably haven't picked up this book because you wake up in the middle of the night with the thought *I need to forgive better*! More likely, you're stressing out, asking big questions. *How am I going to pay my bills? How am I going to heal my body? How am I going to find the love of my life? How am I going to heal my marriage, so I don't break up my family?* And you don't even suspect that it may all have to do with forgiveness.

There are three fundamental premises which you have probably never associated with forgiveness, even if you think you know what forgiveness is about:

1) There are levels to forgiveness;
2) Forgiveness is potentially the most important thing on your to-do list, yet it's often the last thing on it, if it's there at all;
3) Lack of forgiveness is often the reason your life isn't working, even when you've done everything right.

By the time you've finished this book, you will know why forgiving improves every area of your life. You'll know how to make your challenges work for you instead of against you. If you aspire to be a master of forgiveness, wonderful! Because I promise, you'll definitely get there.

You really want to figure out how to make more money, or how to get free of the pain or the disease you have. You want to find a way to heal your relationship, or to have more confidence, so you'll get a better job. Whatever your issue is, you've probably tried a lot of things to solve those problems separately. That's certainly useful, but when that isn't enough, invariably what's missing is the one place where most people never think to look—and that's forgiveness.

How is forgiving the thief who stole my money going to help me get it back? How is forgiving my partner who left me going to compensate for all the years I devoted to the relationship? The truth is, forgiving does not exclude seeking justice and standing up for what is rightfully ours.

Forgiveness is a topic everyone knows about, but rarely does anyone want to become a real student of it, not understanding its value. Forgiveness seems to be that amorphous, religious, or spiritual thing that most people don't consider as a skill that, when mastered, could make life work at last.

The main question is *How do I get my life to finally work*? In this book, you will learn that usually, the reason for your life not working—especially when you've tried everything else—is because the missing piece is forgiveness. Forgiveness truly is one of the most critical universal principles of how to make your life better.

Most people—even religious and spiritual people—have a false understanding of what forgiveness is, and therefore don't know how to apply it correctly. They are trying to build on sand. They end up getting bad results, or no results, and give up on it altogether. This book will help you release the false beliefs about what forgiveness is, and what has been causing resistance to it, so that you can understand it and see its profound benefits. When you start utilizing it correctly, you can heal your life and finally become free.

Just like when there is some deficiency in the roots of a tree, and the branches are not bearing fruit, applying a remedy to the branches will never do any good; you have to heal the blight by giving the proper nutrients to the roots of the tree. Then the branches will flower and bear fruit automatically. Forgiveness is like giving the right nutrients needed at the root of your life.

Forgiveness is an internal state of mind you achieve for yourself, which has nothing to do with others, but everything to do with your happiness. If people are given a choice of working either on their finances, their health, their relationships, or forgiveness, forgiveness often goes last on the list. What if it really needed to be at the top, and then as a result everything else would work out much better?

If you are thinking *Why would I want to forgive? All I want is to be out of debt*! or *I just want to stop fighting with my partner, and I wish our relationship would improve*! the truth is, these problems may well be unyielding because of unforgiveness.

I will show you that you are in charge of what you experience in your life. No one—whatever people may seem to have done to you, and no circumstance, no matter how it appears—has the power to make you depressed, dispirited, disheartened, or unhappy. Forgiving means we have total control over how we think, how we feel, and how we respond, even when we have no control over people and situations.

If we are in a loop of experiencing similar situations over and over, we are probably identifying with our body and personality only. We need to evolve in consciousness—away from the material and into spirituality—which involves recognizing that we are the Divine, or God within, wearing a costume called our name. That shift allows us to see with the eyes of God and to think with the mind of God. God has unconditional love for all Its expressions.

Love encompasses every other quality—including forgiveness—but love has so many different meanings for us that we sometimes cannot fathom what Divine Love means. Loving everything is a concept we have difficulty comprehending, let alone achieving. *If I forgive people, do I have to like them? Do I have to interact with them? Do I need to have them in my life again?* The answer is no. You can absolutely never see them again. But in consciousness you will know that they are an expression of God, and you can honor their divinity regardless of how they act.

There are levels to forgiveness that go hand in hand with our levels of consciousness. When we have internalized and learned to apply these four levels of forgiveness—which I discuss in Part 2 of this book—we can be at peace with the world and ourselves. We can be harmonious and joyful, and be in a place where there is no more blaming, complaining, disapproving, or accusing anyone of anything. At the highest level, you will ultimately realize that there has never been anything wrong—that there is actually nothing to forgive, and you can be peaceful and content.

Isn't that what you really want—to be at peace, in harmony, and happy? It's not what other people do that is hindering us from having the life we really want; it's our own thoughts, beliefs, and feelings.

Forgiveness is not only about the religious idea that you will be a good person when you forgive—as it says in the Lord's Prayer, "forgive us our trespasses as we forgive those who trespass against us"—but this is now a science. Psychologists and psychiatrists have researched what is being activated in our brains when we forgive, and conversely, what happens when we don't forgive and hold onto hate and resentment. It is clear that the neural impulses in the brain impact the well-being of the body.

One of the biggest myths around forgiveness is the belief that just because you forgive people, it means you can't hold them accountable anymore. If they owe you money, or if they have done something illegal, you think you can't seek repayment or legal recourse. *If I forgive them, then I let them off the hook.* That's absolutely false. You can love people and still hold them accountable. You can choose to never see them again, to never work with them again, and also to pursue full compensation, with a heart that has totally forgiven.

There are many more such false beliefs I will be showing you later. Anything preventing you from forgiving is a trick of the ego trying to keep you from evolving your consciousness. When you have been wronged, the place you find yourself in emotionally, energetically—and often even physically—is a very uncomfortable one. Getting out of it would be a godsend! And I will show you how to do it.

At some point, everyone will suffer the backlash of their actions—since energy, once sent out, must return to the place where it originated. This is likely the meaning behind the biblical phrase "Cast your bread upon the waters, for after many days you will find it again" (Ecclesiastes 11:1). Some call it the law of karma. The essence of the energy anyone sends out—stealing, cheating, lying, etc.—will come back eventually.

What people think, say, or do is going to have repercussions. If your response is from a place of anger, retaliation, and resentment, then those qualities will circle back and hit you in the face with more anger and resentment—but they won't affect the offender at all. It's like drinking poison and thinking it will harm the offender.

Even if people do apologize and make restitution, you may still not want to forgive them; you may still think badly of them, not trust them, and want to have nothing to do with them. This shows you that forgiveness is really something you do *for yourself*—for

5

your own inner peace and well-being, and even for your physical health and prosperity. You have full control over your thoughts and feelings, regardless of what others think or do. By the time you're done reading this book, you will understand.

You can either fill yourself up with the poison of negativity, thoughts of revenge, and wanting them to suffer; or you can forgive them so that you are no longer drinking poison. You can still demand justice or restitution, or even put them in prison if that's appropriate—all without any vengeful or unkind thought. As we progress through the levels of forgiveness, you will see how your consciousness can change.

Another piece to pay attention to is that when you withhold aspects of your true nature from anyone—like love, generosity, understanding, acceptance, or compassion—you are simultaneously blocking the pathway for those qualities to come into your own life. When you are unforgiving, you are not *for*-giving.

When you are not expressing the qualities that God (our Source) is always giving you to use, then that channel gets blocked. Source can no longer pour through you. That is why *what you are missing in your life is what you are not giving*. Are you beginning to see that whatever you withhold from another, you are instantly and simultaneously withholding from yourself? You can only have something to the extent that you circulate it.

You not only have to stop drinking the poison of negativity, but you also have to open up the channels through which God pours all of Itself through you, so that you can give godly qualities to others.

If you are thinking *I am giving out love and generosity and appreciation and joy to my family and friends; why should I give any of these positive qualities to that liar and cheat?*—then you have misunderstood the whole Law of Oneness underlying all of creation. You must realize that at our core we are all one—so what you withhold from anyone or anything, you are withholding from yourself.

The whole model of us being only physical is wrong. In actuality, we are spiritual. When a basic premise is wrong, the whole structure built on it must at some point crumble. That is why to some degree, our life is one of stagnation—of *not enough-ness*. If we live from the false premise that we are just a physical person, then the only remedy is to build a true foundation by forgiving every appearance that makes us believe in lack and limitation. That is the deeper purpose of this book.

Personally, I started on the journey of forgiveness through two very traumatic events in my life. First, I lost my husband in a plane crash in Africa, and there was vandalism, too; then, years later, I lost my only son through a willful murder. Both of these tragedies required a tremendous amount of forgiveness work to be done on my part, and the steps I took may well be helpful to anyone who is struggling with similar issues.

What prompted me to write this book is that forgiveness was a central issue in both these events; and yet it's only after my son's passing that I truly understood what forgiveness is about. Everything that happens is an answer to our deepest prayers, which we may well have forgotten. Everything is the playing out of our purpose for this lifetime. It's not that we would ever pray for a murder to take place, or for a plane to crash and be looted before help can arrive—but we do pray for some godlike quality to be activated in us. The Universe brings us the experiences that will fulfill the *soul purpose* of this incarnation—such as self-sufficiency, compassion, trust, love, or forgiveness.

My son had just left for a week's holiday, deep-sea diving among coral reefs. One of the receptionists at his hotel happened to be a woman whom he knew from university, so he invited her out to dinner. He didn't know she had recently broken a relationship with some man, who was jealous and watching her. The man waited in his car for them to leave the hotel, and he drove into them on the sidewalk, speeding off to the main road. They were taken to hospital, and the woman recovered; but my son Albert was in a coma, so I took the next available flight out. For ten long days my hopes were raised and shattered many times. I really thought he would pull out of it when he started breathing on his own, and could be flown back to Switzerland by ambulance plane. When the hospital called for me to come, I fully expected to find him still breathing, maybe awake; but instead I was told that he had had to be put back on life support. I couldn't believe this. He still looked the same, even though he was breathing artificially, with tubes snaking everywhere. The hospital was not allowed to take him off the unit; I was the one who had to do this. I watched him die, as all color drained out of him. That was the hardest thing I have ever had to do in my whole life.

It seemed like my life had ended. This drove me to a depth of hopelessness and a sense of futility that I had never experienced. Also, even if it's hard to admit, I felt that I was a victim. I thought *Why is this happening to me again*? I was already on a spiritual path, since losing my husband in a plane crash. I felt abandoned by God.

The only way out of the downward spiral was to understand, and to forgive.

I tried—really tried—to forgive the best I knew how, without much success. But I kept trying—just as I had done for my husband. I tried for months, and years—because I knew that if painful memories kept coming up I would never get over it. What the repeated attempts gave me was increasing moments of insight, which gradually neutralized the hurt and the feelings of victimization.

Finally, I realized that forgiveness is not achieved by trying, but by the insights you get through your attempts. You can't make forgiveness happen; you can only make it welcome by consistently and sincerely striving.

At some point, this flashback from my childhood came to me: I found myself wishing for the capability to forgive unimaginable harm, unconditionally.

FORGIVENESS IS THE MISSING LINK TO SUCCESS

I was about nine years old, and I had just finished reading a book about one of the 16th-century wars that were continually being fought between Poland and the guild of the Teutonic knights (who came from what is now Germany). The book recounted the story of a commander of his own troop of soldiers, who was taken prisoner and tortured in unspeakable ways for four years. He was finally released when the armistice was signed, but he'd been blinded and his tongue was cut out, so he could not find his way home. After wandering around on foot for ten years, he did finally get back to his family. His sons were no longer children, but grown men. Seeing what had been done to their father, they went in search of the knight who had done this. They brought him back, bound hand and foot, and put a dagger in their father's hand, expecting him to take his revenge. But the father, first lifting the dagger as if to strike, instead cut the cords and let his torturer go free.

I was in tears after reading this story. My one deep desire in that moment was to be able to forgive like that.

As I remembered this, in one instant I saw the reason for the flashback: I understood that way back then, I myself had set up the whole scenario of my son's death—in order to fulfill my desire to become a better, more forgiving person. And all those years later, I was in a situation where that desire could be fulfilled. I only had to choose to do it. In that moment, I *knew* that my son and that woman's boyfriend and I had all agreed, before we were ever born, that they would be the catalysts for my deeper spiritual awakening. The gratitude that arose in my heart—to both my son and to that man—is impossible to describe.

I understood the Divine Love that had made a human being act in a criminal way. I could sincerely thank that hit-and-run driver for his huge gift to me, in accepting the role of the villain. I could even see further back, to the author of the story who sparked my desire to become more than I was. I had discovered the gift hidden in the tragedy. I could only be grateful for the opportunity—which I had actually asked for—to choose a higher response than the grief, anger, and incomprehension I felt.

There was no more need for forgiveness. No harm was done, and there was no victim; we had all agreed to a soul contract that had played out for the highest evolution of everyone concerned. Of that I am certain, even if I don't know how it worked for the others.

So, forgiveness is more than the recognition of a gift. It's also the acceptance of the gift into our deepest Self, so that it becomes the love and gratitude we can offer to others—including to those who harmed us most.

We operate on two levels: the human and the spiritual. A spiritual being can only act in this world through a human being. When we look from the spiritual level, where all beings are pure goodness and only striving to help the incarnated part of other spiritual beings to awaken to their true nature, we realize that every human behavior is only there to help us remember that we are expressing Spirit (God), so that we can act accordingly. I am deeply grateful for that realization.

On the human level, we feel justified about being angry or resentful when we have been hurt in some way; but that feeling is poisoning our own life. Unforgiveness is the cause of so much distress. I know this may be hard for you to hear; you may even feel you could never forgive. That is simply not true. I have proved it for myself, so you can, too.

Wherever you are emotionally right now is okay. You can only start from where you are.

You will know you have truly forgiven when you can sincerely wish everyone the very best, to have every success and to enjoy all the abundance they may desire. That's lifting your consciousness a little closer to the level of Spirit, which sees no wrong. You then will have chosen a higher response than you ever have previously—one that is congruent with your true nature.

This deep forgiveness is a process of love and recognition of the true essence of every person; and you don't have to contact the person at all if you don't want to do so. There is nothing for you to do physically; it's your consciousness that does all the work.

Remember, forgiveness isn't just a destination, it's a journey—a way of life. Be gentle and patient with yourself—and enjoy the ride!

If you just want to forget the traumatic event or the issue, and not think about the person any more, hoping the suffering will go away because "time heals anything"—know this: *Time never heals anything*, unless you take steps for the wounds to heal. Things will change, but unless you consciously *activate* the best parts of yourself—those aspects that reflect the harmony, love, and wisdom of the Source of Life—things can't actually get any better.

Even if people mostly manage to get their lives together again after a traumatic event—where clearly, and humanly, there was someone to blame—it's not often that they arrive at the understanding that the event was actually a catalyst for their evolution to the next level. At this high level, we are able not only to forgive, but also to open our heart to the perpetrator and become grateful for the growth and spiritual understanding we would never have had otherwise.

The purpose of this book is to allow you to see the mechanics of the various stages of forgiveness that we go through, which are intimately linked to our level of consciousness. It is my desire that you will be helped out of any unforgiveness which is poisoning your life—whether you realize it or not at this moment. Step by step, if you're willing to take the journey, you'll enter an understanding of how life really works "from glory to greater glory of that which endures" (2 Corinthians 3:11).

In Part 1 of this book, I will be taking you on a journey of really understanding the various aspects of forgiveness and unforgiveness. We'll see how to find those elusive places when we think we have forgiven everybody and everything, yet our life is still not working.

In Part 2, I will be describing the different levels of forgiveness and giving you exercises to actually work with any issues of unforgiveness that you may have, to resolve them progressively at higher and higher levels, until you feel that they are no longer a problem for you.

While Part 1 is basically informative—where you are invited to really contemplate the ideas that may be unfamiliar to you, and to consider accepting them at least as a possibility of being the truth—I would encourage you to take some more time with Part 2. Really sit with the exercises and practices. Make them real and meaningful in your life, and you may find you have had some insights that I have not even included in this book! I hope that you experience some outcomes beyond what you would have ever thought possible.

Forgiveness is more powerful than our justice systems, prisons, or conflicts. Forgiveness healed my life, and it can heal yours. Condemnation and prison sentences can never really do that.

This book is meant to help expand your awareness, to help you realize that there is nothing I can teach you or give you that you don't already have within you. If my words become a catalyst for you, it's because you already knew it all along at an unconscious level, and it has simply been brought into your consciousness. For that, I am profoundly grateful.

PART 1

THE MANY FACETS OF FORGIVENESS

CHAPTER 1

WHAT FORGIVENESS IS AND WHAT IT ISN'T

The Story of a Rwanda Genocide Survivor

During the Rwanda genocide, a woman watched her son, her only support, be horribly tortured and killed in front of her eyes, along with most of the inhabitants of her village. She, along with many other women, was spared, and years later, the perpetrators of this massacre were brought to justice. The survivors were invited to the court hearing. Among the prisoners, she recognized the man who tortured and killed her son.

All the women present were surrounding the prisoners, insulting and even attacking them; but she quietly went up to the man she recognized, and said, "What is done is done, and no one can do anything about it. But rather than perpetuate the hate and abuse that only leads to more unhappiness, I want to say there is no hate in my heart for you, or for any of the others. I forgive you for what you did; and if you're willing, I want you to become the son that I lost. Come into my house as my son; do not suffer in prison. Suffering can only cause greater suffering; and I want to stop that cycle, for you and for me."

She asked the judges to release the man into her custody, in her village. While all the other prisoners were led off to prison, that man was released into the care of the woman, who adopted him as her son.

THE BENEFITS OF FORGIVING, AND THE CONSEQUENCES OF NOT FORGIVING

If you think forgiveness is just a theory, or an elusive thing dreamed up by some church or religion, you're wrong. Yes, most religious paths advocate it, but for believer and nonbeliever alike, forgiveness is the missing piece to solving many problems and making life work. It's one of the most practical ways to eliminate pain, suffering, and struggle. Even from a selfish point of view, forgiving our enemies has huge value. Who wants to stay in distressing or painful feelings, when the recipe for a joyful life is as simple as forgiving everyone for everything?

In order to truly forgive, we must first be *prepared* to forgive. The first half of this book is the preparation. It's not just education or information; it's also inspiration and motivation. We pull weeds from the soil, turning it and adding nutrients to it, so that when we plant the seeds, they grow. In the same way, we must cultivate the soil of our soul in order for it to be fertile ground for this powerful practice of forgiveness. In the process of attempting it, we get insights and an expanded awareness, which starts the healing of the trauma experienced. Then we don't just let go of the issue; it eventually lets go of us — because it can't live in the high frequency of an expanded awareness.

Whatever the problem is — whether it's money issues, problems with friends, colleagues, our partner, health, or well-being — forgiveness is going to help resolve it, while blame and vengefulness will exacerbate it. Becoming a forgiving person can completely transform your life.

What Forgiveness Is Not

Perhaps the biggest reason for not forgiving is because we don't really know what forgiveness is and what it isn't. I want to start by busting some of the false ideas and teachings about what it means to forgive. Clarifying what forgiveness is not will help to eliminate some of these ideas, and make it easier to forgive.

- Forgiving doesn't mean you are excusing people's actions, or not holding them accountable.
- Forgiving doesn't mean there is nothing more to work out between you, or that everything is okay now.
- Forgiving doesn't mean you have no more sad or painful feelings about the situation.
- Forgiving doesn't mean you have to tell people directly that you have forgiven them; it's strictly personal to you—an inside job.
- Forgiving doesn't mean you have to keep that person in your life.
- Forgiving doesn't mean you should forget that the incident ever happened.
- Forgiving doesn't mean you are weak, or a doormat. Quite the contrary!
- Forgiving is not some religious idea of loving everyone—even cheaters and abusers—to earn your way to Heaven while your life on Earth is wretched.

Forgiveness is not about avoiding the thoughts or memories; it's not about trying (unsuccessfully!) to forget what happened. Memories will keep coming back. It's about releasing the negative charge that the event or situation holds in place. If we are at all conscious, we realize we have to somehow get over it, and put it behind us. We begin to see that holding onto resentment doesn't serve us. Unforgiveness is not useful, because it's not hurting them, but us.

Here is what forgiveness does and doesn't do:

- It doesn't change what happened; it changes your perception of the event.
- It doesn't necessarily change the other person; but it definitely changes you.
- It doesn't necessarily change the material outcome; but the spiritual outcome is what matters most.

I want to show you what happens when you forgive, and what the consequences are when you don't. This is by no means an exhaustive list, but it probably indicates many things you are experiencing right now, and it will help you see where you are positioned.

The nine core benefits of forgiveness	Nine core consequences of unforgiveness
1. Increased well-being	depression, constriction
2. Increased health	disease, sickness
3. Increased abundance	lack, debt
4. Increased power	powerlessness
5. Increased clarity	confusion, tenseness
6. Increased peace of mind	stress, worry, anxiety
7. Increased confidence/competence	overwhelm, feeling defeated
8. Increased mindset of growth/expansion	closed, contracted mindset
9. Better, healthy relationships	troubled relationships

When forgiveness is the missing piece, as I've pointed out in the introduction, that's often why our life is not working. When you understand what forgiveness truly is, you will start to clear the blockages standing in the way of the clarity you need to live the life you want. You'll be free from victimhood. You're going to feel more motivated to have those difficult conversations with your boss or spouse.

How to Deal with Issues

If you are struggling in any area of life—feeling confused, or not empowered enough in a relationship to speak your truth—maybe the remedy isn't merely going to therapy, or taking another class to learn to speak better. Even if these are good steps to take, they may not be all that's needed to get you to where you want to be. What if I told you that there may be some deep issues of unforgiveness, some past core wounds blocking you, preventing you access to the power you need to stand in your situation and clearly speak your truth?

For example, perhaps you're in a job you hate, and you feel there is something more for you, but you don't know what it is, or how to go for it. You've taken programs, and you've read books on how to make more money, but it's still not manifesting. In many cases, what's blocking your clarity is some judgment, shame, or unforgiveness you have for some part of yourself. You don't accept yourself fully, and as a result, you can't get in touch with the parts you reject, which actually contain what you need. When you learn how to forgive these places, suddenly you will get the clarity and the empowerment you've been seeking. What was blocking your desires starts to dissolve, and ideas will flow more easily.

Forgiveness can help you clear up that problem with your boss, because you will finally see that what you are really reacting to is not your boss, but some old wound about authority figures, and a perception that you are a victim. You've been trying to improve your efficiency in the workplace, but you've never addressed the forgiveness side of it. When you really work on forgiving those aspects of yourself—what it is that makes you feel wounded—and then forgive the people you feel have judged and repressed you, *that's* what's going to give you the power and determination to take a stand and ask for that raise, or resolve whatever your issue is at work.

Forgiveness is both an emotion and a behavior; its real value lies in the change it brings to our mindset, behavior, and emotions, and therefore to our health and well-being. Wherever you are right now, whatever you are feeling, whatever you are going through—and I really want you to take this in—who you are, where you are, and what you are feeling right now are all absolutely natural and normal. Maybe you're really angry, and that's okay. I'm not going to tell you to get rid of your anger; in fact, I give you permission to be as angry as you want! You have the right to be angry about what was done to you. Maybe you're really sad, and you feel hurt and betrayed. That's okay, too; you have a right to feel that. You have a right to feel every feeling that comes up, and every feeling is okay—it's just energy expressed. And if it's a painful feeling, why not metaphorically take it in your arms and hold it in your heart? It's a part of you that's in pain. *It needs love, not rejection.*

If it were your little son who got his hand caught in a door and was screaming with pain, would you say to him, "Stop crying, get over it, it's nothing"? Of course not. You would take your child in your arms, hold him close, and say, "I know it hurts, and I'm sorry! I don't know when the pain will stop, but I will hold you, love you, and stay with you until it does!" That's how we need to treat every hurt, and every painful emotion that comes up.

WHAT FORGIVENESS IS AND WHAT IT ISN'T

Forgiveness can be defined in terms of changes in motivation. We become less motivated to retaliate, less motivated to maintain a distance from the offender, and more motivated by conciliation and goodwill. When we endeavor to forgive a person who is not close to us, we think of forgiveness as reducing or eliminating resentment or the wish for revenge. But in close relationships, it means more than just removing the negative. We become less motivated to stay estranged from people, and more motivated by feelings of kindness, regardless of their actions. In family dynamics and in close relationships, forgiveness will not only get rid of negative emotions, but move us towards positive feelings. We don't have to change our emotions, but if we don't change our *response* in some way, unforgiveness can wreak havoc on our physical, mental, relational, and even spiritual health.

In a psychological study, people were asked to think about someone who had hurt or mistreated them, and while they were doing that, their heart rate, blood pressure, muscle tension, and sweat gland activity were monitored. The study proved that their blood pressure and heart rate and sweat increased. The subjects reported that they found just *thinking* about the incidents was unpleasant and stressful. It made them feel angry, sad, anxious, and less in control. Next, the subjects were asked to imagine forgiving the person. Then, all their physical symptoms decreased down to normal levels. Therefore, it would seem that forgiveness may free a person from being imprisoned in a state of vengeful emotions. Forgiveness will thus yield many benefits, such as reducing stress, improving the immune system, and diminishing heart problems.

That link between unforgiveness and negative health symptoms comes from the fact that hostility is a central part of unforgiveness, and hostility has been found to have the most devastating health effects, such as the risk of cardiovascular disease. Letting go of a grudge helps free a person from hostility and its damaging consequences.

Who Do We Need to Forgive?

Forgiveness breaks down into two categories: forgiving ourselves (which means being forgiven), and forgiving others. What are the unforgivable parts of ourselves, and the unforgivable parts of others? And of course, this includes everyone—whether living or dead—because ultimately, it's all about healing ourselves.

When we are at fault, we need to forgive ourselves, and also to ask for forgiveness from another. That's often difficult, since it demands a level of vulnerability that our ego is not prepared for. This occurs when we are at the "normal" level of consciousness, where we want to protect our self-image. Even when we aren't able to see ourselves as at fault, we are still not at the level of what Source is. We need to forgive those aspects that are anything less than the wholeness and the perfection of Source.

You may have heard of Dr. Hew Len, a psychiatrist in charge of a psychiatric hospital in Hawaii who cured all the criminally insane inmates using the ancient modality of Ho'oponopono healing. He took 100 percent responsibility for all the ways those patients showed up for him, forgiving himself for those aspects, without ever even seeing the inmates. When he was completely healed, he found that they were healed as well—and the facility was shut down for lack of patients.

Usually, we start overcoming the natural resistance to forgive when we can see a benefit for ourselves. The situation we are struggling with—at work, with our kids, or with our finances—has its roots in some early trauma that we've forgotten, but didn't forgive.

When we don't forgive—both emotionally and mentally—we start creating immune system deficiencies that cause pain and diseases, disrupt our social life, and often create financial debt. This happens because our attitude is that people *owe* an apology or redress of some kind. Forgiving is a cognitive and emotional process that eradicates chronic hostility, anger, rumination, and their adverse effects. It also takes away the feeling of anyone owing us anything. There are countless examples of people unable to get out of debt, but as soon as they started truly forgiving those they held resentment against, abundance started showing up. Either the debt was erased, or they received an unexpected financial windfall that took care of it.

True joy—as distinct from happiness—is one of the greatest benefits of forgiveness. You are happy when you receive a gift, when someone shows you appreciation; but the deep joy you feel welling up from inside—sometimes for no apparent reason—is the effect of the soul's attribute of *seeing no wrong*. We forgive in order to experience that joy—the freedom from all the negativity that unforgiveness represents.

Modern research has shown that forgiveness is linked to mental health, showing reduced anxiety and depression, fewer major psychiatric disorders, fewer physical health issues, and lower mortality rates. Psychology now accepts that chronic stress is bad for our health. Stress relief is probably the chief factor connecting forgiveness and well-being, because forgiveness allows us to let go of the stress between people that is a burden on our systems.

In addition to stress, "toxic" anger, which is deep and long-lasting, poisons all our systems. When we can release it, our muscles relax, we have more energy, our immune system strengthens, and surprisingly, it can even help to rebuild self-esteem. While there is nothing wrong with "healthy" anger, which is short-lived, when we are continually angry at injustices whether personal or in the world, we end up not liking ourselves very much. When we courageously face the hurt that happened, and offer energetic goodwill—to the person who hurt us, or towards world events—we change the way we see ourselves.

We all have had situations that were painful, distressing, even terrible. But we can think of them now without the emotional charge they had in the beginning. They are just things that happened. We can look with equanimity on the events and the people concerned.

For example, some time ago, a car bumped into mine from behind, and I felt my neck being dislocated. I had it checked out, and the hospital said I would need one of those stiff collars around my neck for months. Right from the start, I decided to hold no resentment or blame; it was just something that happened. The next time I went for a check-up, I was told that the healing was going much better than expected, and that it wouldn't be long before the collar could be taken off. The doctor was amazed, but I knew that it was my mindset of peacefulness that had allowed my body to fully focus on healing, instead of most of its energy going to fighting the toxins generated by an angry and unforgiving attitude. It took only a few weeks—not months—before I was okay again.

Unforgiveness leads to anger, frustration, and resentfulness—impacting physical, emotional, relational, and financial well-being. Every time we think of the people who hurt us, we feel really bad. Then we are stressed, in a fight-or-flight mode, so most of our energy is directed to the muscles. There is very little left to fuel our immune system, so it becomes deficient, and we end up catching every bacteria or disease that normally would have been rejected. What's more, we are totally in ego identity, with no spiritual understanding.

Furthermore, an unwillingness to forgive encourages a victim mentality, which results in depression and disempowerment. Our ability to appropriately respond to events and circumstances is impaired. Whatever our challenge is, it's never against us, but *for* us—in terms of us having to become more inventive, more pro-active, more resourceful, or more decisive—growing us in some way.

If you don't quite understand this yet, it's okay. Just allow for this possibility, and we will discuss it in more detail in later chapters.

Forgiving is a journey we embark upon; it's never an *I've done it once and it's done* kind of thing. It's a path—filled with emotions, unhealed wounds, and fears—so it may be a good idea to seek help along the way, in order to gain clarity around mental or emotional blind spots. On our own, it's often difficult to see the long-term benefits of forgiveness for our health, social life, and finances. The short-term benefits include the improvement to our character—how we show up in our interactions with others in a kinder, more balanced way. Getting support—either friendly or professional—will help us to succeed more quickly. It's always a good idea to seek assistance in doing anything that's difficult for us to figure out how to do. Any way we end up doing it, it's a journey that will take the time it needs to take. And it's only about ourselves, not really about anyone else. We need to be patient, considerate, and kind. It's not possible to beat ourselves up into well-being!

WHAT IS FORGIVENESS? AND HOW DOES IT WORK?

We need to change the way we think about forgiveness. It's never condoning a misbehavior or crime. What has happened—whether it's lying, abuse, or crime—is always reprehensible, and we call it what it is. It's never okay when it's harmful to yourself or to others. So it's legitimate to feel hurt, to be resentful, and to be angry. Allow yourself every feeling that comes up. It's okay to own each emotion, and even to allow it to intensify as it moves us up the scale of emotions. For example, first you may feel depressed and powerless, and then angry, wanting revenge. Then you might be blaming others, as you feel your disappointment and frustration. Allow yourself to feel it all, so that the energy moves to whatever feeling comes next, each to be naturally replaced over days or weeks by the next feeling—until you reach a neutral point. Then you will have processed all the negative feelings, moving into tolerance, and further up the scale. Thus, forgiveness means moving through the feelings, not repressing them. We eventually get back to our essential nature.

We need to disassociate the action from the person, because the person is and always will be an expression of Divinity, yet has used life energy in harmful ways—through ignorance, conditioning, false beliefs imposed by others, or self-created lies. Forgiveness does not preclude common sense. Of course, if anyone breaks the law, or murders or harms another, there are consequences to that. Discernment, however, allows our consciousness to rise above the human perception, to see people in their inherent innocence.

Only people unhappy at their core commit acts of abuse, terrorism, murder, or other unacceptable behavior. The soul knows this. As we identify with our soul rather than with our personality, we can say that what happened was not okay; but we can also see that the behavior was coming from flawed humanness, not from the highest wisdom of the perpetrator's soul. We can see that this person was placed in our reality as an opportunity to reach higher wisdom. The soul allows for forgiveness; our ego doesn't need to be the forgiver.

The ego, the human part, ties itself up into knots trying to forgive stuff that is really bad on the material level. Unquestionably and materially, such behaviors need to be stopped. But when the *soul* rather than the ego is the one that forgives, the personality is no longer in charge. Simply *allow* the forgiveness, and Divinity will do it for you. All you have to say is: *I allow those who have blamed and wronged me to be forgiven.*

Notice how much easier and lighter this feels, when you take yourself out of the equation.

If there is some misconduct that needs to be forgiven, let us consider that maybe the whole scenario was designed for us to gain a more expanded and spiritual understanding of life.

Engaging in prayer and meditation, with sincere intent to forgive, and listening to guidance to show you how, the material benefits will naturally emerge.

With that connection to Spirit opened up again, we realize that what we really, really want is to have peace, joy, and love! When we understand the principle that what we are missing is what we're not giving, we're now going to radiate love, peace, and gratitude to everyone and everything—without exception.

When we withhold love, joy, and peace from anyone, then more love, joy, and peace can't come into our own life. We have blocked a channel of goodness and abundance to ourselves. We start realizing that others are actually only another dimension of us. Therefore, the more we bless everyone else, the more we open our channels for blessings to flow to us.

The reason this strategy will always work is because every aspect of it lies squarely with us: We are not dependent on anyone for anything—not for apologizing, returning, restoring, or regretting. Everything depends on us and our alignment with our soul, which is unconditional love and allowance. We give permission for our soul to be in charge of doing everything that, as a material personality, we are unable to do. Therein is the peace and freedom we crave.

Spirit pours all of Itself, all of Its aspects, into every one of Its expressions. We need to let them out as the thoughts, words, feelings, and actions—which become visible manifestations in the world. If we deny anyone—including ourselves—any divine aspect, like love, kindness, joy, or compassion, then stagnation results. A pond stagnates when there is no outflow and inflow of water. Circulation and energy movement are laws in our three-dimensional world; without circulation, the flow of energy is interrupted, and on some level, torpor and death occur.

When we don't give love, we're blocking love from coming to us. When we don't wish abundance for another, we block our own abundance. We block our own healing—mental, emotional, or physical—when we don't intend it for another, resulting in emotional and energetic debt, and often leading to financial debt as well. However, we can reverse the process.

Energetically send good wishes instead of mental insults to the neighbor who has been a pain in the neck for years, and just watch how quickly your recent neck pain starts to dissolve!

One example I can share of how circumstances can change is from my own experience, when my husband died in a plane crash—and my whole life of over 27 years in Africa was shattered overnight. It took me years to truly forgive the circumstances of my husband's passing. The strangest thing was, I thought I had forgiven. I didn't even realize that the process of forgiveness wasn't completely done.

> *The plane had crashed on take-off into swamps that were difficult to access. The people of the nearby villages were the first on the scene. They took machetes to get into the cabin to loot it, without any regard for the passengers—some of whom may have still been alive, as in fact my husband was. They took all personal belongings, including watches and rings—and because they had to do it fast, they cut off people's hands.*
>
> *When the police finally arrived, the only person still alive, but by now in a coma, was my husband Marc. He was taken to a hospital, and I heard about the accident hours later, from the police.*

At the time, my grief was overwhelming. I was afraid of thinking too much about what had really happened. The pain was too much—the anger, the blame, and my judgments of the looters brought up unspeakable images. Then of course, I had many ready-made excuses—having to deal with moving back to Europe, finding a place to live, finances, taking care of my son's education, finding a job, etc. These were all real problems, but still they were excuses for not doing the introspection. Talking about this to anyone was too painful, so I never did. The pain and emotions around it became locked inside me.

When I started writing this book, I was brought to the realization that I had been avoiding the whole subject for years. I therefore hadn't truly forgiven. The process of getting there involved bringing into full consciousness why I was avoiding thinking and speaking about it. I thought my pain and suffering came from grief and loss—when really it was from unforgiveness regarding everything I knew about the accident, plus everything I suspected. It required a lot of introspection, reading, and studying spiritual material, until my perceptions gradually began to change. With help, I expanded my awareness of how things really work, and then all the residue cleared up.

When something is too painful to talk about or even to think about, it's a definite indication that the forgiveness process isn't complete. All the things we avoid thinking about we need to bring into awareness, so that we can understand what's going on and why. Wherever we don't want to go, whatever we want to avoid at all costs, that is exactly the place we need to go into, if we're going to heal—ultimately to become totally liberated. Look at introspection as a powerful tool that helps you to forgive and move on.

All of my judgments were the places I didn't want to go. Those who looted the plane never thought of giving help; they were unfeeling, uncaring, out for what they could get, cruelly mutilating the passengers to get every bit of gold they could find. The idea of what had been done to Marc was too painful to contemplate. I was feeling guilty and ashamed about having those judgments, and I did not see that guilt and shame would lock them into place even more. Only by looking deeper under all the beliefs and implications, many years later, was I able to truly see that I was not being honest with myself.

The key issue here was that I wasn't willing to be fully authentic and frank about what really happened and how I really felt. I came up with a story, a reason why I was refusing to talk about it. I said that I didn't want others to feel judged; I didn't want to project this onto a whole culture, when it was only a handful of marauders who did it. But what I was really afraid of is how facing the facts would make me feel—or what it would mean about me: that I was a powerless victim—judgmental, angry, and unforgiving.

Trying to forgive finally brought my unforgiveness into full view. You can only heal what you allow yourself to feel. The energy I could not allow myself to feel then, for rational reasons, became stuck in my body. If I wanted to heal this trauma that was keeping the pain alive for over 35 years, I had to decide to actually do it.

When we have a judgment against any person or group, in order to heal it, we have to be willing to be courageous enough to be honest about it. We need to see that there are still places where we have real judgment about someone or something, including ourselves. If we have any shame or guilt around it, this stops the process of forgiveness.

Whenever we avoided thinking about a painful issue in the past, what were the results? Chances are, they were never positive!

For me, turning to spirituality—and continually trying to forgive—did not work. I didn't see that I was not totally honest about what I felt. I thought I was a good and forgiving person. That's called a *spiritual bypass,* which is a tendency to use spiritual ideas and practices superficially, in order to sidestep unresolved emotional issues and psychological wounds.

It's really difficult, not to say impossible, to do deep introspection work on our own; outside assistance is often needed. I was lucky enough to get that help. Only when I fully realized the dissonance between where I was and where I wanted to be, did I understand that I was protecting my egoistic nature. I wasn't seeing from the perspective of my soul; I was afraid of being judged by others. I didn't want to think about it, speak about it, or be honest with myself. That's a sure sign of a sense of separation from Divinity.

It took a few weeks of sitting with my feelings—fully feeling them, and accepting them as a part of me. All those feelings had been protecting me during the time I was not strong enough or connected enough to my soul to be able to feel them without any judgment. They allowed me to be more open to the truth of my being, more unprejudiced and fair, more broad-minded and forbearing. When I stopped rejecting those shadows—understood and accepted them—they released their gifts. (Shadows are intrinsically positive qualities that we have judged as bad, due to some experience we had early in life—such as asking for a second scoop of ice cream and being told *don't be so greedy*. We will expand on what shadows are in Chapter 3.) It was those gifts that finally allowed me to bring everything I knew and everything I imagined about the crash to the surface, and to feel it all, in order to transmute the trauma.

This kind of work is not easy, because we can get lost in the feelings. To keep from becoming totally overwhelmed, it's necessary to take aside a part of yourself as a witness who is seeing the trauma from the soul's vantage point. I had witnessed myself several times when I felt I was in a deep dark hole. Since I knew this process would be particularly difficult, I asked a friend to hold the space of witness for me.

Whatever the story is that we tell ourselves about why we don't or can't forgive, it's never the truth. It's some form of protection of our ego—of who we think we are in the world—and we think it will preserve our safety, security, and material well-being. The deeper meaning of any challenge is to make us realize that we have been living in a world that's too small for who we really are. We have prayed and affirmed what we want, and who we want to be in life; but our desire can only really manifest when we become the person we are meant to be—when we're living our highest vision.

The truth is, there is nothing that can't be forgiven, and everything must be.

At first, our reason for forgiving could be just that we want more of the goodness of life to flow to us. That may at first seem egotistical, but let's consider this: Whatever energy is sent out must return to its creator, to complete the circuit back to Divinity. When we send out negativity, it gathers up similar negativity floating around, generated by human beings, and returns to us—amplified many times. We must then purify it before it can complete the circuit back to Source. If we don't, the negativity continues to sabotage our life. But when we send out positive thoughts, words, and actions, then amplified good energy returns—blessing our life. Even from a self-centered perspective, it's worth our while to forgive!

Forgiving means refusing to live life in a state of anger, resentment, bitterness, or antagonism. It's something we do so we can have peace of mind, and the space to think more positive thoughts. The situation may not change, but our perception does. The kind of thoughts we're having changes, and therefore, we change.

Psychological, Medical, and Spiritual Aspects of Forgiveness

We can choose a state of consciousness that's not dependent on outer circumstances. Because it's not possible to hold two opposing thoughts at the same time, studies have shown that holding a thought for 90 seconds or more starts the magnetic attraction of similar-frequency thoughts. Negative thoughts attract pessimistic ones. While when we consciously switch to happy, pleasing thoughts, additional enjoyable ones are drawn in, lifting our mood. Therefore, we are not allowing negativity to anchor itself to create stress, which adversely impacts our health. This is how we can bring back wholeness and peace, making us free.

Even at our most dense physical level, what medical literature in general suggests is that from a psychological and neurobiological point of view, forgiveness represents a positive, healthy strategy to effectively overcome a situation that otherwise would be a major source of stress for the individual. More specifically, a constant attitude of forgiveness is associated with a diminished recourse to medication and alcohol. Forgiveness of a situation is also associated with a reduced heart rate and its physical symptoms.

We are told by science that a negative attitude and chronic emotional distress erode health, alter cardiovascular reactivity, impoverish sleep quality, and stimulate the production of stress-related hormones. Over time, these are associated with the development of clinical conditions such as depression. Conversely, forgiveness promotes well-being, cardiovascular health, and may even increase survival rates. Unforgiveness shuts things down and creates all kinds of mental, emotional, and psychological negative feedbacks. The benefits of real and true forgiveness are literally built into our biology.

Consciousness Is Cause

In its essence, forgiving has to do with consciousness. It is a spiritual principle, not a surface material issue. It's a need to forgive some part of *ourselves*. It's about opening a channel where we have been blocking the outpouring from Source—denying it to ourselves and others. It's about letting go of what does not serve us. It's about bringing to full consciousness what was unconscious.

Anything we struggle with is pointing to an area that needs to become more conscious, so we can sit with it, acknowledge it—be with it. The first question to consider is *What if this doesn't mean what I think it means?* What we have made it mean may not be true, and our misperception is locking it down even deeper. Everything that's being triggered and brought up by a situation was already in us from past experiences in childhood; but when life flows smoothly, such feelings can easily remain unseen. We don't even realize that this is going on inside. To make us conscious, to remind us of the hidden negativity that needs to be released, challenging circumstances have to arise.

See if you can find a place in your life where you had a problem with someone, and now you don't; maybe you're even friends again. That was forgiveness. Something happened, and now you don't have any anger or pain or fear around that situation or person. Can you identify a place in your life where that occurred? Take a moment to think about it. Sometimes forgiveness happens by grace. Most often, it has to be intentional.

Now, if you thought of an event from your own life, let's take a closer look. See if you can identify some of the things that you did, or didn't do, that led to forgiveness. For example, did you share your feelings? Did you release them? What did you say, or refrain from saying? We'll get much deeper into this in each chapter, and eventually we're going to practice on the areas where you still have unforgiveness. For now, it's very valuable to identify hurts that were healed and resolved, that are no longer a problem for you.

If you're still alive and functioning, odds are that forgiveness has happened more than once in your life. When you can see that it's happened, you will develop faith that it can happen again. When you see that you've actually done it, and how you did it, you will realize that you're not as far away from being good at it as you may have thought.

In my own life, I know I have been moved into a more expanded place because of forgiving the murderer of my son, and I can be truly grateful for the awareness which allowed me to do that. As I described in the Introduction, insights opened up, giving me a higher understanding of how that man was only playing his role in a scenario that the three of us had set up before we were ever born; in essence, there was nothing wrong, and everything was in divine order. When that got through to me, I was given the additional grace of remembering that as a child I had actually desired the ability to forgive unforgivable wrongs.

The point is, so often, when a really painful event occurs, we say, *I couldn't have created that, or asked for that—that's insane*! We don't realize that when we wish for a certain quality—for example, patience—do you think that patience will just magically descend upon you? No! What will happen is that we will attract people who irritate us, people who push our buttons—so that we will have an opportunity to practice the quality we wish we had, and then we'll become really patient. When we've embodied it—become a master of patience—then those people will either leave our environment, or we will no longer be irritated by their ways.

When I asked for the ability to forgive when it seemed impossible, I was too young to realize all that. Nevertheless, the Universe heard the request, and decades later, it was granted. I still had the choice either to take the opportunity to grow, or to stay in grief with a desire for revenge.

Every challenge we meet is an invitation to become someone better than we were before, and that's how life works for our highest good.

Real, true forgiveness comes from the heart—from a deeper spiritual understanding. It's far more than just making everyday life more comfortable. It's about developing a more spiritual understanding and making a more conscious connection with Divinity—our true Self—where there is no sense of being wronged in any way. Spirit has nothing but love for everyone and everything.

That means we do our best to bless and appreciate everyone and everything, including ourselves. The highest good for others is the highest good for us, too. That's a forgiveness shower we can take every night. Over time, we'll notice less and less of a charge when thinking of the offender, until we get to a place of neutrality. From there, it will turn to the positive, and we'll start feeling compassion, understanding, and tolerance. That's how we know we have truly changed.

You may not be there yet, and that's fine. As you continue reading, a lot of healing and growth—and expansion and activation of your power—can happen. Even before you get there.

WHAT'S POSSIBLE WHEN WE FORGIVE

In any situation, the experience we're having is created by our mindset. When we blame, worry, get angry or frustrated in our most intimate relationships, we feel dejected and hopeless, and even our health suffers. But when we decide to have an open and constructive conversation with the people we love the most—instead of mulling over what they did, or what we thought they did, and why they did it—the whole issue starts looking very different and much less serious than it initially appeared. A better understanding of what was really there, and what our role in it was, and what it can be now, is essential for a better outcome.

Looking at your own life, can you find an example of when you were really afraid of what someone you loved—your partner or child—would think of you if you did a certain thing? Something that, in your heart, you knew was the right thing to do? Did you refrain from forgiving a person who had caused hurt to someone you loved, because you thought that your loved one would then despise, reject, or abandon you? In any case, how did staying in the state of resentment make you feel? Did you at some point, in your heart, become more peaceful about the whole issue? Then that would mean that some forgiveness took place. Can you identify how, and why? Were there any conversations or actions that made it easier for you? Finding those pieces will enable you to redo the process with any other problem you may have now; eventually, you will be so clear and empowered, you will have forgiven everyone and everything on every level, with joy and peace flooding your world.

Conversely, maybe there was an occurrence in your life where you did not forgive. What were the consequences? Think back to why you objected, and examine how that has been detrimental in certain areas of your life. There are valuable lessons to be learned, which will prevent future distress.

In the reviews you just conducted regarding your own life—those instances where you found that unconsciously, accidentally, or by grace, you did indeed forgive—notice that the result was an expanded sense of joy, freedom, and well-being. You were able to look past what had been done to you, and overcome your fears for the future.

We are all expressions of the Divine, and at that level, we are one. In that place of forgiveness, notice how you can now more easily recognize that the people who hurt you are also an expression of the Divine—and maybe in your heart you even feel a sense of connection to them, although you may not be with them anymore. Or, possibly, from where you are right now, the last thing in the world that you want to believe is that they are divine, or that you want to be one with them! But take heart and have faith: As you do the forgiveness work, you will not only begin to realize their true divinity and your oneness with them; but the eventual healing of a belief in separation will lead to you having more joy in your life.

Try this experiment: Every night, bring the guilty party to mind and search for what there is about the individual or the situation that is positive—something that moved you forward into a greater understanding of what life is all about. Silently send this person compassion, appreciation, and forgiveness.

You will eventually find that you have acquired more clarity than before. You'll start to see the possibilities that could occur when you finally are able to forgive. Start envisioning what life could be like in every major area. Don't leave out spirituality, which is the connection with Spirit from which all goodness flows. Without the energy and qualities Divinity is gifting to you, nothing would be possible.

The fact that we are having a challenge is an indication that mentally and emotionally, we have been living in a world that is not expansive enough for the greatness of the Spirit within us. We have been praying for more abundance, for finding the love of our life, for having a closer connection with God, yet we have not really been *actively going for it*. It's time to *get to work*—on giving up false beliefs and on letting go of limiting thoughts and habits, while at the same time activating the truth. The deeper truth is, we are an undistorted expression of the Divine—powerful, brilliant, harmonious, joyful, peaceful, and abundant. Prayer and faith without the accompanying required action yields no results.

Now that we know what forgiveness is and what it isn't, and what the benefits and the consequences of not forgiving are, we can see that for many of the problems we have been struggling with, forgiveness is the answer.

Let's reach for a better, more expanded life. It's our challenges that show us where we need to up-level our thoughts and beliefs, to start acting *as if we were* that peaceful, joyful, and abundant being. Of course, we don't want to do stupid things, like spend money we don't have, or risk health issues; proper discernment is a quality of Spirit we also need to cultivate.

What would life start to look like, when all the consequences of holding blame and resentment have been resolved—by forgiving everyone involved, and forgiving every aspect of ourselves? What would life be like, when there is no more stress, worry, overwhelm, discouragement, or powerlessness?

What remains is joy, peace, ease, clarity, and empowerment.

Isn't that a picture worth forgiving for?

CHAPTER 2

WHY WE RESIST FORGIVENESS

> *Without forgiveness, life is governed by an endless cycle of resentment and retaliation.*
> —Roberto Assagioli

Let's bust some of the myths that have been passed down through our families, upbringing, and religion. We are up against so much internal resistance to forgiving—showing up as distractions, pre-judgments, objections, laziness, and reluctance to change. Of course, we would much rather have others conform to suit our needs—which almost never happens!

When we consider the word *forgiveness*, what's the initial reaction? Maybe it's just a really nice thing to do, for spiritually minded people? Or perhaps we think that it's something only a fearful person would do? Perhaps only a wimp forgives. Is saying *I forgive them* the easy way out? Those who think that have never really attempted it. Forgiveness requires great courage, with a lot of self-reflection.

We resist forgiving those who have hurt us, betrayed us, cheated us, broken contracts, etc., because they don't deserve it. They are bad, and they must be punished. But we need to ask: *Is my resentment affecting the perpetrator in any way?*

If we choose to be ignorant of the true aspects of a painful situation, we'll easily find reasons not to forgive. Keep in mind that most people don't have the intention of hurting someone else. They just do what's best for them. Obviously, that does not excuse misconduct or criminality; but realizing it can stop you from reacting violently.

I'll share an example here from my own life:

> *I was waiting for money due to me, but suddenly had to travel to Timbuctoo, so I asked a friend to collect and hold the money for me. When I got back, I found that my friend had received it, but spent it. She was truly sorry and promised to return it as soon as possible.*
>
> *I was so angry, I didn't listen to the reasons. I called my friend a thief, and decided I would never forgive her, nor ever trust her again. I went off, feeling upset and badly hurt. Later, I found out that my friend's child had had an accident; she'd had no money for medical costs and so she used what was available at the time—the money entrusted to her.*
>
> *Now, my degree of distress changed direction. I felt the need to be forgiven for the part I played in that scenario, by refusing to listen. I could have taken it peacefully, I could have asked for her reasons, and then there would have been no issue. With understanding and compassion, I could admit that the responsibility for creating the problem lay mostly with me, while at the same time I could still hold my friend accountable for repayment.*

On the relative level—i.e., the human level—there are situations we either like or don't like. On the absolute level—that is, the spiritual level—*situations just are*. We mostly identify with the relative level, which always changes, depending on geographical location, upbringing, religion, gender, nationality, culture, and even our mood in the moment.

WHY WE RESIST FORGIVENESS

Maybe we have reduced our idea of God to a God who punishes sinners and rewards those who do good. But in the Scriptures, we are told (and I'm paraphrasing) that God's sun shines on both the saint and the sinner; His rain falls on the just and the unjust (see Matthew 5:45)—which means that God gives His gifts equally to all. God is Source Energy, not a person who takes sides. God is Law—the spiritual law of goodness and perfection. When we align with spiritual laws, the outcome must be good; when we act counter to them, the outcome becomes painful. These results are not because God is punishing us, but because our actions stem from a relative (human) level of consciousness. It's time to go higher, to the absolute (spiritual) level.

Vindictiveness, or seeking revenge, is the old, human law of "an eye for an eye and a tooth for a tooth" (Exodus 21:23–25), not the spiritual law of love and forgiveness. As the saying goes, if we keep acting according to this outdated human law, we will all end up blind and toothless!

Has revenge ever righted a wrong, or made us feel any better in the long run? Yes, temporarily, we may feel some relief and a release of energy when hating people or lashing out at them verbally, or even physically. We need to somehow express all that anger and hate, which is better than repressing it and letting it fester for months or years, causing depression and many other issues. However, let's be sure to act it out when we're alone—pounding pillows, crying with rage, and calling the person names. This healthy expression of emotions makes for a valuable catharsis; it releases those totally normal feelings, and keeps us from acting out against the offender, which would compound the injury and make the situation worse. If we take time to reflect—if we are at all conscious—we will see that lashing out or taking revenge would just add another wrong to the wrong already done. We would then have a new sense of guilt or shame come up, for which we would have to forgive ourselves.

If we are judging others—they are mean, selfish, dishonest, weak, stupid, crooks, or liars—it is because there is some aspect of that judgment within us. As I say that, you may be thinking *I am not mean, dishonest, or a liar, like they are; so how can you say that?* Your reaction is understandable—and I am not accusing you of that—but it's still important to understand that if we're triggered, it's because that energy is in us. We may not be acting it out, and we may not recognize it; it's locked away in our unconscious.

Right now, you don't need to understand it fully, but it's essential to know that this is so. If you did not have that quality in you, you couldn't resonate with it and feel that judgment towards someone else.

It's the same principle that happens when there is a row of violins with strings, each tuned to a particular frequency. When you strike one string on one violin, the same string in the other violins resonates. When you take that string away, or tune it out on all the other violins, and strike that note again, none of them will resonate. They don't have that frequency. So, when you resonate with the frequency of a quality—whether positive or negative, either admiring or judging—then you have it in you. That's all you need to know for now, but we will get into this concept much more in the shadow discussion in Chapter 3.

Initially, forgiveness is a decision we take from the intellect, because we know we should, or we want to find relief. Making that decision is better than nothing; but it probably still leaves us with a residue of resentment, anger, or sadness. Ideally, from that intellectual position, we could gradually move to seeing the person as a misguided child of God who deserves our compassion, which opens the way for our transformation into a more aware and better human being, possibly grateful to the individual for being the catalyst for that transformation. From there, there's more work to do. For now, we must first overcome the basic resistance to starting on this powerful journey of forgiveness.

WHY WE RESIST FORGIVENESS

WHY SO MUCH RESISTANCE?

There is always resistance to forgiving. The ego creates from a position of resistance. That's not the way the Source of our being creates. Our soul doesn't resist anything. It just sees things as they are. When we are angry at our partner for cheating, the soul just sees someone who has gone to seek happiness elsewhere. Since the soul is omniscient, it also sees all the possible outcomes that depend on our response. We are in charge of finding the highest response possible. Endeavoring to tap into the expanded perception that our soul has of the event, and to act accordingly, will result in a positive outcome for our highest good.

It's normal not to want to forgive inexcusable behavior; but a negative reaction turns us into a victim, affecting our ability to appropriately respond to the event or circumstance. We feel completely innocent. We see the wrongdoing as something that was done *to* us, so we take no responsibility for it.

Other reasons for unforgiveness might be that the anger makes us feel alive and in control; there is some pay-off in not forgiving. It moves us out of victimhood and powerlessness; there can be a lot of power in feeling angry and vengeful. It can feel great, because it's a higher state of consciousness than victimhood and depression. The key is, feeling vindictive, wanting revenge, and wanting people to get their just deserts is very human, and a necessary path on the spectrum of emotions. Many spiritually minded people might be quick to say that vindictiveness and revenge are bad. They skip that stage, trying not to feel those feelings. When the feelings have not been fully felt, however, they will keep coming up to be resolved. So we might as well do it now—in the moment, when we are really upset—and get total liberation from them.

It's undeniable that some of us find it easier to forgive than others do. New studies have established that there is a correlation between the development of a certain part of the brain and the willingness to forgive. There were studies conducted with a group of volunteers, which measured the volume of gray matter in the part of their brains called the anterior superior temporal sulcus. They were then given a number of different case histories where forgiveness was necessary—with information not only about the damage done, but also about the perpetrator's intention and mental state—and then they were asked to give their moral judgment in each instance. It is already scientifically well-established that when the outcome of an action and the intention are conflicting—as when there is unintentional harm done—people tend to focus mainly on the intention. And this new study has established that from an anatomical point of view, the more developed that part of the brain was in these subjects, the less blame they attributed to the wrongdoers.

CORE OBJECTIONS AS TO WHY WE DON'T FORGIVE

There are some core reasons why people object to forgiving. In my research and practice, I've discovered there are 13 most common arguments people put forward. That's not to say there are not more, and you may straightaway think of some I haven't mentioned. I want to start with the three biggest ones, which are:

1. Forgiving means I condone the behavior;
2. Forgiving means I am letting people off the hook;
3. If I forgive, they will do it again.

Below are the most common arguments invoked as legitimate reasons for not forgiving; but when you really examine them, they don't hold water.

1. **Forgiving Means Condoning the Behavior**

    That is just not true; there is no law that says you can't forgive *and* hold a person accountable. When we forgive, we're not saying that the wrongdoing was okay, when clearly, it was not. That would feel inauthentic.

    Look again at the example where there was forgiveness in your life. Did that happen because you condoned the person's behavior? Did it occur because you made it right that the person lied, cheated, stole, or betrayed you? Or was it because you did your own inner work, you released that individual, and thus you reclaimed your power?

    We also have an example in the Scriptures. When Jesus was speaking to the woman caught in adultery and to the men who were going to stone her, he said to them, "let him who has never sinned cast the first stone" (John 8:7) and they all slunk away, leaving no accuser. Jesus did not condemn her either, but neither did he condone, saying, "Go, and sin no more" (John 8:11).

2. **Aren't I letting them off the hook?**

    No! What they think and do is their responsibility; what you think and do is yours. This objection basically means that we want people to pay for the misdeed, to be punished. We are adding our feelings of anger and revenge to the harm already done, magnifying the negativity already present. We are in victim consciousness, identifying with our body and personality.

Rising into our spiritual identity — into the Truth of who we really are — will make us see that wrongdoers act from the level of their physical personality. The physical self is not who they truly are. If we look at the material realm as reality, we are forced to identify ourselves with our position on the material plane as well. Just as others have made mistakes, so have we. Focusing on the harm done to us condemns us to staying at the material level, where we'll experience the effects of our own mistakes and guilt. With a higher perception, what we are really doing is liberating ourselves from the consequences of our own errors. It is up to others to liberate themselves from the consequences of their own mistakes.

3. If I Forgive, They Will Do It Again

Indeed, they might! But has *not* forgiving ever stopped anyone from doing it again? We are only responsible for *our own* behavior, not someone else's!

If we think that to forgive means giving permission for the wrongdoing to happen again, that's not a true understanding of forgiveness. They might do it again or they might not — whether or not you forgive. But you can get free of your anger, and by forgiving, you could be the very one that prevents it from ever happening again. By expressing true and complete forgiveness, you might create the condition in consciousness where someone does really change. Think of all the pain you could prevent in the future, not just for yourself, but for anyone else who could be harmed by the actions of that individual.

Let's continue with the rest of the 13 most common arguments people have against forgiving.

4. I Don't See Any Value in Forgiving

This is where we are caught in a strong sense of separation, and simply don't see any point in forgiveness. We are in victim consciousness, a slave of the offender, who has the power to make us angry or resentful. By transcending victimhood, we begin standing in our humanly generated power. By establishing strong boundaries, we will never let that be done to us again.

This is a good step, but there's more. It's actually the opposite of real power, the opposite of real peace. We are never free as long as we feel that we have to protect, and defend, and set up walls against another. Of course, we take common-sense precautions. We lock our doors, we don't leave credit-card information lying around, and we don't pretend not to see what is obviously unethical behavior. To accomplish forgiveness, we need to let go of the consciousness of being unsafe, victimized, or attacked in any way. If we let the actions of others rob us of equanimity and joy, we have given our power away to them. Forgiving brings karmic freedom from the residue of our past and present actions. There are many hidden benefits, which we don't always see at first. We need to love ourselves enough to make sure our perceptions align with Truth. Then we are the ones running our own life.

5. I'm Afraid to Feel All the Pain of That Experience

We try to forget the trauma because it's just too painful to remember the suffering—whether it's physical, psychological, or emotional abuse. The brain doesn't know the difference between emotional and physical pain; so we believe that to open ourselves to emotional pain is equal to putting ourselves in physical danger, where we might not survive. When we repress our feelings, the energy hasn't disappeared; it's still wreaking havoc—in our life, our body, our relationships. Unless we release the negative charge of past experiences and patterns, we will continue recreating them. Keep in mind that releasing doesn't mean forgetting. We have learned valuable lessons, and we don't want to forget those along with the incident.

In order to heal, we need to feel the initial pain again, and the negative feelings towards the people involved—no matter how afraid we are of going through the process. It's okay also to feel a sense of guilt and shame. Living with those feelings stuck inside compounds the pain. For instance, whenever I thought about what was done to my husband, while still alive on that plane, I thought it was un-Christian to judge and hate those people. I hated myself for hating them. I was afraid to feel the anguish, the grief, and the rage towards those who did those terrible things. All of that interferes with the ability to forgive.

If the incident was not too traumatic, it's absolutely possible to forget it, and so we think we have nothing to forgive. Yet whenever the people involved come to mind, we don't really like them, and we don't know why. When we have an instinctive dislike for people we don't even know, it may be that their energy field triggers some area of unforgiveness in us—either known or unknown—which needs healing. Resolving such feelings can be done by identifying them, seeing the gift they have brought, and integrating them. But of course we can't heal what we don't feel. I will be giving you tools on how to do that in Part 2 of this book.

6. I Want Them to Make Restitution for What They Did

This denotes an exclusive focus on the offender. We want rectification or compensation—an apology, reimbursement, taking their words back, etc. Then, and only then, would we even consider forgiving. But remember, we have no control over anyone except ourselves. Most times, the redress, if and when it's made, has no influence on whether we forgive or not.

7. I'll Betray My Loved One Who's Been Hurt if I Forgive

When someone we deeply love has been harmed or offended, it creates suffering. We feel we must not forgive, since that would mean we are betraying that loved one. Or, it might mean that this loved one won't forgive us if we forgive the wrongdoer.

In truth, we are afraid of being rejected by our loved ones. What that amounts to is that we are judging ourselves as unlovable, unworthy, not good enough. This is the part in us that needs to heal, to be integrated. We are projecting a judgment upon others—when really, we don't know how they would act. Our loved ones might end up being grateful for us modeling a higher response than they are capable of having right now. Failing to stand for our truth—for what we know, deep down, is the right thing to do—would be co-dependent behavior we should avoid. Quite the reverse of betraying anyone, as we work on freeing ourselves, it also creates the right conditions for those closest to us to do the same. It's a blessing for ourselves and for our loved ones.

8. Forgiving Those Who Hurt My Race/Culture/Religion Is a Betrayal of That Group

This reasoning is similar to the one above. Basically it's subordinating what we know is right, to what the group thinks is right. We have the belief that the group knows best, when our own inner guidance tells us that what it is advocating is wrong. If we don't forgive those who hurt our group, then we remain subject to the pain—the karmic influence, and the baggage—from our own race, culture, or religion. What we're doing is staying stuck in the identity of our group, thus subject to the limiting beliefs and laws of that group and its karma. By doing so, we keep ourselves trapped in the pain and suffering.

For example, if as a Native American or a black person, we hate white people and feel that they have hurt our tribe, we will continue to be subject to that hurt. If we forgive, we can transcend our group identity and karmic baggage. We will not only free ourselves, but we can become a light that helps to liberate others in our group as well.

When we don't forgive, it's often because of a fear of rejection by that group. In extreme cases, it can lead to death. Look at what Jesus was standing for, in the face of his tribe, his religion, and the whole of the Roman Empire. And yet, who was right? The individual, or the group?

9. It Means We Have to Be Friends, That We Have to Have Them in Our Life

Of course not. We are all free to choose who we want in our life and who we want our friends to be. That has nothing to do with forgiving them. There are plenty of people in the world we don't want to have dinner with, even though they've done nothing to us. There are many family members we never care to see, even though they've done nothing to us.

If people are dishonest or abusive in any way, either on a personal or business level, we can disassociate their personality from who they really are, and forgive them—while still pursuing justice. At the same time, we can permanently cut ourselves off from any further dealings with them. That is honoring ourselves for who we really are, taking good care of ourselves and not letting anyone take advantage of us or devalue us in any way. We endeavor to see them through the eyes of Spirit, which sees only spiritual perfection.

10. I Tried to Forgive Them Before and It Didn't Work

When this is the case—that it appeared to backfire, leading to more hurt, harm, or other negative experiences—first, as I've already said, understand that we are not responsible for how anyone else acts. Our responsibility is to decide only how *we* will think, feel, and act.

It could be that the ensuing result was for some other reason, something about which we are presently unaware. Or, perhaps we didn't really forgive. It was one of those lower-level ego-based intellectual practices, paying lip-service to what we thought we should do—so it didn't come from the heart, and the inner work clearly wasn't done. It doesn't mean that your forgiveness didn't work. It's just not yet complete. We may have only cut the top of the weed off; the roots are still there.

By the time you're done with this book, you're going to know how to truly forgive. You're going to know specifically why it didn't work, and you're going to know how to reverse all of that permanently.

11. I Forgave Them and They Did It Again!

Forgiving is not a way to stop or prevent bad behavior; we forgive in order to free ourselves from the anger, resentment, frustration, or sadness it's causing us. So if we are in this situation, it obviously relates to us. We have to ask: *Why do I keep letting this person hurt me?* It's not about the other person; it's about us. *What's the payoff? Where do I need to forgive myself?* Because when we let others keep hurting us, it's because we don't believe we're worthy or valuable enough. We don't respect ourselves.

For example, a man cheated on his wife, but she still loved him and so she forgave him. Then it happened again, so she thought she shouldn't have forgiven him. But did she really look at all the reasons why it happened? Could she have had some responsibility for this? Did she speak up the first time she felt something was not right, or was she afraid of his reaction? Did she suspect, but merely hoped it wouldn't happen again? That's co-dependence—shadows of feeling unlovable or unworthy, which she still needs to integrate. Did she clearly set boundaries for what she expected and what she holds as important? Did she truly realize what was missing in the relationship for him to cheat? Did she change some things in her own life in response? Did she accept him as he was, respect him, understand his needs, and support him? As she looked within, she realized that the reason for him cheating again wasn't because she forgave, but for some other reason. What was her pay-off for not speaking up? Where does she need to forgive herself for believing she's not good enough?

In a relationship, no one is ever totally right; no one is ever totally wrong. Understanding that we carry part of the responsibility is necessary. We need to forgive ourselves, which frees us to also forgive the other person. If we're in a relationship where we're truly being hurt or abused, we might consider getting out of it and working on ourselves from a distance, because we also need to honor ourselves by not accepting being repeatedly belittled or abused. Letting ourselves be hurt or abused is never acceptable.

If you don't quite understand this yet, it's okay; we're going to talk more about it later, so you can finally and fully forgive yourself.

12. The Person I Need to Forgive Has Passed On, So How Can I Forgive?

When people who hurt us are no longer living, we may feel there is no need to forgive, because it's too late; we can't do anything about it. We may think they don't exist anymore, or that they are now back with God, and don't require our forgiveness. That's a misperception of what forgiveness really is: Forgiveness is strictly for us and for our own well-being. It's about our perception of people, and our relationship to people within our own heart. Whether they are alive or dead really doesn't matter.

For our own peace of mind and happiness, we need to forgive, so that we no longer have anyone—alive or dead—making us feel uncomfortable or sad.

13. I Don't Trust Religions That Talk About Forgiveness; They Have Caused Great Suffering

A religion that speaks of forgiveness—like Christianity, and most others—has been a source of great pain and suffering for many; so if we reject that religion outright, along with it goes the whole idea of forgiveness. But if we take the time to discern what the true teaching of a religion is—as opposed to what people think it is, and how it is being misapplied—we will find that there is a universal Truth underlying all religions. We need to strip away the dogma and church laws that were imposed upon the true teachings. There were also misunderstandings that occurred through mistranslations of the ancient texts, and inaccurate transcriptions. Sometimes there was willful removal of certain parts of the Scriptures that were not to the liking of the authorities in place, such as what happened during the Council of Nicea, in AD 325. There is a real need for discernment, so as not to throw away the baby with the dirty bath water. We need to search for the universal Truth resonating deep inside, and live according to that—not according to what anyone else says.

CHAPTER 3

WHY FORGIVENESS WORKS AND WHY IT DOESN'T

When Chris Carrier was ten years old, he was abducted near his Florida home, taken into the swamps, stabbed repeatedly in the chest and abdomen with an ice pick, and then shot through the temple with a handgun. Remarkably, he was still alive. Hours after being shot, he awoke with a headache, unable to see out of one eye. He stumbled to the highway and stopped a car, and the driver took him to the hospital.

Years later, a police officer told Chris that the man suspected of his abduction lay close to death. "Confront him," suggested the officer. Chris did more than that. He comforted his attacker during the man's final weeks of life and ultimately forgave him, bringing peace to them both.

If we ever think we can use forgiveness as a mechanism to control someone else's behavior, that is when it fails. When we take the other person out of the equation, accept the situation, focus on ourselves, and give the compassion and love needed in that painful situation to the one who's been hurt, that's when it works.

Forgiveness is not just a nice option, but a necessity—if we don't want to stay in suffering. It's not just saying *I forgive you*. It's acting in a way we wish the other person had acted. It's expressing the opposite quality to the one the other person showed. In order to do this, we need the assistance of the Higher Self (God). When we humbly ask for that help, it is given. The higher part of us can step in *as* us, and then we just let It operate Its magic. Our ego resists forgiveness, because it fears we might lose love or respect—even self-respect. We might be judged as weak, undependable, powerless. We may think nothing will ever change.

The top five reasons for forgiveness appearing to fail are:
1. We are using it to control or change people, to get back what they took, or out of fear of the consequences.
2. We are using it to feel superior, to hide vindictiveness, or to avoid feeling like a victim, or stupid, or naïve.
3. We are just going through the motions, but our heart isn't in it; we believe just saying it is enough.
4. We are doing it from the ego, which renders forgiveness impossible, because we're not humble enough to ask for divine help.
5. We haven't remembered to forgive ourselves for the shadows we have created by our judgments.

Every instance is different, so many times there will be a combination of several of these reasons, or you'll have your own specific reasons. Thinking forgiveness has failed because we have not received the full fruits we expected—meaning that we are still angry, sad, or not at peace—could be accurate, but it doesn't mean it has failed. It just means we are not done with the forgiveness process. It's not a failure; it simply hasn't been completed.

If we're harboring sadness, resentment, and anger, we can't be at peace. We are still in blame mode, upset *because* another person did this or that, *because* this or that happened. That's blaming someone or something as the cause of our feelings. People and circumstances are never the cause of our feelings. Those were already in us from past unresolved hurts, and simply brought to the surface by what happened now, to be transmuted and released.

Feeling emotions is part of the beauty of human life. We are meant to feel all of them and let them pass through, making room for the next feeling that comes up, as we go up the vibrational scale. A vibration can be physical—like, say, the vibrations from an earthquake—but it can also be emotional, describing the frequency of a person's emotional state. In other words, emotions are energy in motion. Energy just is; it's neither good nor bad. Our judgment makes emotions what we like or dislike, accept or reject. With that understanding, we can not only forgive the event, but be grateful that it allowed us to transform some negativity that was hiding within us.

Humanly, we like to be in control, to know that we are managing things. That works most of the time in our everyday life. When it comes to forgiveness, we don't realize that the same rules no longer apply. We have no control over what anyone else does. Letting go of control is not easy, since it's the exact opposite of what we're used to doing.

We may try to use forgiveness as a way to boost our ego, to feel superior. Pride enters in, to hide our real pain. But the pain is still there, repressed. We need to become humble, willing to feel every emotion—no matter how bad—for that shift into forgiveness to occur. Start where you actually are. It doesn't do any good to skip those first stages of being angry and devastated, just as you don't want to skip the stage where you're using training wheels to learn how to ride a bike.

When forgiving hinges on getting something, achieving an outcome, manipulating someone, that's when the ego has taken control. As we abandon our agenda, let go of all control, that's when suddenly it works. We feel better, more peaceful. We are letting our soul be the doer.

When Peter came to ask Jesus, "How many times must we forgive?" Jesus answered, "Seventy times seven" (see Matthew 18:21–22), meaning *as long as it takes*! Forgiveness is a way of life. We're healing and clearing multiple layers.

We have often heard that whatever triggers us, we must have within ourselves. Say someone has been dishonest and stolen from us, and we think *I must have that energy of dishonesty within me for this to happen*! And haven't we all, on some level, not been totally honest—even with ourselves? But that did not cause the event. It happened so that we could either discover that pocket of dishonesty in ourselves where we are not walking our talk; or, so that we could see some aspect of ourselves, such as holding judgments. Recognizing whatever it is that is not in alignment with our soul, we then have the opportunity to correct those behaviors.

Naturally, we strongly resist the idea that we ourselves could have those aspects we judge and so much dislike—such as laziness, selfishness, aggressiveness, weakness, or stupidity. That's not to say we are in fact like that. These judgments about others represent moments in our life where we rejected those parts of ourselves and made them wrong or bad. Then we projected them onto others. Anything negative is just energy we have misjudged. It's not necessary to blame anyone. Blaming anyone is never constructive. Energy can be used in two ways, constructively or destructively. The label we put on someone's behavior doesn't change the energy; it just makes our life either happy or unhappy.

Lazy, in its constructive aspect, is taking a well-deserved rest!

Stupidity may simply mean having a different perception.

Aggressiveness can become power.

The truth is, our goal is to be happy and fulfilled. When we are happy, we can't at the same time blame anyone or anything. Anyone who blames or wrongs another is, deep down, an unhappy person. If we really can't see in ourselves any aspect of dishonesty, if we have always been totally honest even with ourselves, and therefore carry no responsibility for the event at all, it may have happened just so that we could realize the judgments we have and heal those—which will make us more loving and compassionate, evolving us to a higher level.

Everyone and everything that shows up in our lives is a mirror of our *true* judgments and beliefs, not the ones we *claim* to have. It is those beliefs and judgments that we need to heal in order for our circumstances to change.

USING FORGIVENESS TO CHANGE, MANIPULATE, CONTROL OR GET SOMETHING BACK

Making people or events responsible for our feelings locks those feelings in place. Do we really want them to continue plaguing us? Was there a time in your life when you have felt sad, or happy, for no reason? Did the feeling stay, or did it quickly dissipate, to be replaced by a different emotion? When we attach a reason to an emotion—like a person or event—every time we think of the person or the event, the emotion resurfaces. Feelings dissipate much quicker if we don't blame someone or something for them.

For example, our partner is disorderly, aggressive, and uncaring. For a time, we put up with it and forgive, hoping for a change that never comes. We leave the relationship, and start another one, but after the first few weeks the next person proves to be just as bad, if not worse. We notice that we always attract the same kind of person into our life. Maybe it's time to look at why we allow this kind of behavior. What's the fear? That this person will leave, and then we'll be alone? That we're unlovable? Not good enough? Where within ourselves do we have that quality of disorder or aggressiveness that we so much dislike?

It's likely that we're beating ourselves up about something all the time! *That's aggressiveness*—towards *yourself*. Maybe our mind is scattered, disorganized—starting things and never finishing them. Do we plan our life as to how we want it to be, and commit to it? Are we easily swayed by circumstances? Do we love ourselves, appreciating our abilities? Are we taking good care of ourselves? That's the place to start changes.

We need to forgive ourselves for those mistakes, and look at those shadows. Whatever we judge in someone else is our shadow. It's energy that we have misjudged because of a painful experience early in childhood, which is why we are now rejecting those aspects. It's time to see the shadows as divine energy that we have misjudged, and now, we can welcome their gifts. We'll start to attract people who don't have those behaviors, once we have integrated that energy. I will explain in detail how to do that towards the end of this chapter, but don't fast-forward yet!

A common underlying reason for not forgiving is fear—lack of a backbone:

> *Let's take the example of Mary, and Claire her daughter, who disapproved of her mother's remarriage and became overtly hostile towards her new stepfather. Mary never said anything, afraid of rejection from her only child.*
>
> *When her stepfather died, Claire persuaded her mother to make her a beneficiary of her stepfather's insurance, even though she had no legal right to it. That done, Claire refused to sign the documents unless she was given the lion's share. Now, finally, Mary was outraged, and didn't give in. The insurance couldn't pay unless everyone signed, so the entire sum was lost for everyone. Mary's first reaction was I forgave her for being so mean, and even shared the insurance, and that's the result!*
>
> *In truth, the financial loss was not the result of Mary being forgiving; rather, she was weak in not demanding respect for her*

marriage much earlier. She again feared rejection if she refused to give Claire the insurance. Her apparent forgiveness stemmed from fear, and a desire to manipulate Claire into being a loving daughter. It didn't make her more discerning; it didn't change her in any way. She did not protect her own interests before making Claire a beneficiary, and consequently suffered financial loss.

Mary finally reflected on the real reasons for the loss, and recognized the real cause: her own weakness and fears. Now her growth process could start. She clearly saw her own responsibility, and desired to become a more evolved, responsible person. That sincere wish to change herself triggered an understanding that, had it not been for Claire's bad behavior, she would not have gained her current backbone. Mary could release Claire of all blame, but not necessarily trust her in the future. Appreciating the maturity and character she now had, she saw that it all happened for her ultimate good.

We are always gaining something with every challenge that we go through. There is always a grander plan.

USING FORGIVENESS TO FEEL SUPERIOR, OR HIDE VINDICTIVENESS

Imagine a scenario where Jack helped his Uncle Bill to repaint his house. Bill was willing to pay for Jack's time, and they agreed on a certain sum. But once the job was done, Bill didn't pay, and asked Jack to wait until his next pay day. Jack was okay with that, and came around at the end of the month. But Bill procrastinated. So Jack waited, reminding his uncle of the debt many times, with no result. Now Jack was getting frustrated and angry, and suspected

Bill simply didn't want to pay. He remembered that he had a reputation for being untrustworthy, but since Bill was family, Jack hid his vindictiveness, so as not to create a situation where Bill would be exposed.

The longer this went on, the angrier Jack became, but he didn't say anything, ashamed of having been naïve for not putting the agreement in writing. He was also angry at himself for letting himself be taken advantage of, afraid of people knowing how foolish he'd been. Keeping it quiet even made him feel good about himself. He felt better than his uncle, even if deep down, he knew that wasn't true. Jack was really protecting himself from being judged. Yet he was feeling constricted, unhappy, and tense. To free himself from all that, including the feeling of a false superiority, Jack needed to clarify his confused feelings, and stop rejecting them.

The issue was not about Uncle Bill at all. It was about Jack healing his own shadows, triggered by Bill's behavior. Jack no longer recognized himself. More than what Bill did to Jack, it was Jack's own feelings about himself and the situation—his lack of discernment to not set up proper safeguards—that were hurting him. With a contract, he could have demanded to be paid, without any anger or resentment. That's forgiveness from the heart. He could absolutely have no further interaction with Bill, apart from demanding what was rightfully his.

So, when Jack did the necessary self-reflection, got clear, and forgave himself for his role in the problem, his fear of being judged was gone and he could now confront Bill openly and demand his due without blame, shame, or apology.

OUR HEART ISN'T REALLY IN IT; WE BELIEVE JUST SAYING IT IS ENOUGH

In the case of physical harm or abuse of any kind, it's really hard to forgive, especially if it was intentional. It doesn't even feel right to forgive; the individual doesn't deserve to be forgiven, and needs to be punished. We were taught to forgive; we know we should, so we try, but our heart isn't in it.

At first, we are deeply hurt and want the individual to suffer. We have no way of getting even, so we say we forgive, while hoping something bad will befall that person. We hope God will render punishment. Resentfulness builds up—even vengefulness. That's the first level—a valid stage—but we don't want to stay there too long, as it's a very uncomfortable place. It will not make our life a happy one.

We need to carefully examine every aspect of the situation. When we are blaming anyone for cheating or for being abusive, could we have encouraged it? Could we have stopped that behavior right away? Maybe we neglected to take action when we saw early signs, because of fear of what would happen if we stood up for ourselves. Maybe we persuaded ourselves that the person didn't really mean it. Perhaps verbal abuse lasted for years, and we just took it, because we didn't want the kids to witness fights in the house, or because we didn't want our children to be brought up with a single parent. We may have thought we were being a paragon of forbearance; but really, we lacked courage and self-esteem, giving our kids the example of a weak, undeserving and powerless parent—instead of a strong, powerful, and forgiving one. In every instance of personal abuse, there is usually some responsibility we need to take for being mistreated. Furthermore, if we blame ourselves for being foolish enough not to have seen the signs before, and see that we were gullible enough to believe the lies, it's time to forgive ourselves for that.

Gradually, we realize it's our own feelings which are causing the distress, so we decide not to hold a grudge. We don't want to let people harm us once, and then hold us hostage for life. Taking responsibility is a way out. This is when forgiveness works. We acknowledge that we have been victimized, and that nothing is our fault. We forgive ourselves for feelings incongruent with the dignity of our soul. When we raise our consciousness by identifying with Spirit, we know we were never touched by such behavior. We can seek justice, but at the same time, in our feelings, we're ascending the stairway towards true forgiveness one step after another, getting insights, and moving towards a higher understanding.

The greater truth is that each individual always remains an expression of the Divine. Realizing this is when forgiveness becomes a practice of surrendering, turning it over to a Higher Power that can forgive *through* us, when humanly we are unable to do it. Humility and vulnerability play a large part in this. Every action we take, whatever it is, always moves us forward a little bit, even if it appears to be a step back.

In the examples I have just given, there runs the thread of our human personality, the ego, being in charge. The shift needed in our perception is to recognize our divine nature. Really, it's the energy of God running the whole show. Forgiveness doesn't work until we fully hand it over to the Divine.

FORGIVING FROM EGO IS IMPOSSIBLE; WE'RE NOT ASKING GOD FOR HELP

Another reason why forgiveness appears to fail is because we've looked at only one aspect of the incident—for instance, betrayal. Usually there are more facets to explore. Feeling betrayed means our ego is wounded, so we think the ego must forgive. Trying to forgive from our personality is like cutting off only the top of a weed without pulling out the roots, and wondering why it's still growing. For instance, maybe we were trusting because the person is of a certain culture or religion. Other issues will then emerge. Doing the inner work on even the most obvious part of the problem will move us forward vibrationally, allowing more insights into other potential explanations.

A proper diagnosis of where precisely the blame lies is critical. Who, in addition to the perpetrator, needs to be forgiven? We need to forgive every aspect that might come up as we look deeper. Perhaps we discover that if it was a man or a woman who betrayed us, now we show distrust towards the whole gender. Maybe the distrust was already there, from some childhood experience—when your father just left one day and never came back; or your mother didn't keep her promise of taking you to the playground, and you felt betrayed. If you developed a mistrust of all men, or of all women, now there must be forgiveness not only for the particular person, but also globally, for the entire gender.

Sometimes, because we are trying to forgive a present situation that is deeply rooted in the past, we are unable to fully forgive until we have addressed the primary core wound. Without addressing that primary experience, those negative emotions or beliefs often resurface, and won't fully let go.

A great example of this was a client of mine, an absolutely brilliant woman who couldn't make any money. Whatever she tried never worked. She knew she had all the knowledge and the skills necessary, so she couldn't understand what was blocking her. In our conversation, we uncovered an unforgiveness of her father; she didn't want to talk about him, so her resentment was obvious. Even as a child she was outstanding, and her father was always pushing her to achieve more. But he punished her for the slightest mistake so she couldn't trust herself, couldn't trust her own brilliance. She couldn't trust herself to do things right, so her business was stagnating.

Gaining that clarity was one thing; but forgiving was quite another. She turned to God for help in forgiving her father—from the standpoint of the adult she now was, not from the hurt-child perspective. Her father wasn't intentionally mean; he really wanted her to become more successful than he was. He had also been punished by his parents, and had never been shown a better way to correct mistakes. He was a victim of his own upbringing. In this way, she found great compassion for him and a deeper understanding of his viewpoint. Formal forgiveness became unnecessary, with the love she now felt for him.

Within a few weeks, her business started turning around, and it wasn't long before she was really successful.

When we skip a step in the forgiveness process, we don't integrate that level. It doesn't become a part of who we are. Think of your own life now. Can you remember a time when your father or mother promised you something really important for you, and then didn't do it? Did you let yourself feel all the sadness, disappointment, and even anger? Or did you repress all that, not liking having those feelings? They are your parents, after all! Suppressing those feelings didn't make them go away, right? The feelings were still in you, ready to flare up at the slightest pretext.

Any feeling that comes up is legitimate. We need to feel and acknowledge them all. We don't take our feelings out on others, but we do give ourselves permission to fully feel them in the moment, so that the energy can move and dissipate. Otherwise it gets locked in the body and festers. Don't get lost in the feelings and start thinking things like *What's wrong with me? My life is really bad, nobody loves me,* and *I'll never amount to anything*! Instead, step back and simply observe all the emotions. It's surprising how quickly we can't even find them anymore, when we consciously allow ourselves to feel all those "bad" feelings. Just watch them as an observer; let the emotions flow.

After the death of my son, a family member wrote me a very nasty letter, ending with *I suppose condolences are in order, so here are mine.* I was so hurt, I didn't reply. I burned it. That was really hard to forgive, but I sincerely tried. I thought I had managed, but when that person contacted me again about some issue between us, all the old feelings of mistrust and hurt came up again.

I knew I had to change. With help, I worked through my feelings. Finally, the whole problem no longer bothered me at all. What I had wanted to come from the outside—peace of mind—I had achieved internally. Within a few weeks, the issue was resolved in the way I had always wished for. It was just and equitable for the other person as well.

My process went like this. First, I didn't want to forgive, or have anything to do with that individual. Later, I was willing to forgive, but didn't know how, so I knew I needed help. It's always a good idea to ask for help—and most importantly, to request God's help—when embarking on addressing a forgiveness issue that we haven't been able to resolve on our own. I finally saw how to change my interpretation of the situation. It starts with realizing who we really are, and who everyone is. Being focused on forgiving a misdeed keeps us focused on the wrong. Instead, I included this person in my daily prayers—consciously sending wishes of happiness, success, and wealth—which I hadn't ever done before.

At first, it felt inauthentic. I wasn't feeling it. I persevered anyway, and eventually the words I so much resisted saying became familiar to my ego, and it no longer rejected them. If you keep saying the words, they become known and habitual, and the resistance drops on its own. That practice opened me up to seeing that she and I have the same Source. No human in this world is my source, because there is only One Source. No person can hinder the unfoldment of God in my life. Then I saw that since both my real life and nature are divine, and because my Source has infinite abundance, then whatever seems to be taken away materially can never diminish what I have spiritually. All I need can be given to me from Source. That realization, I knew, was the reason for that person being in my life. For the first time ever, I felt true freedom. That was true forgiveness. I understood that my true nature is Spirit, so all the demands were being made on Spirit (God). Thus God, as me, could meet every demand, and handle any situation.

It took time for me to fully understand this. We don't always apply what we have learned from one occurrence to another. Each time is a little different. Be patient with yourself.

In any instance that needs forgiveness, let's ask what is the positive, opposite energy of that pain or hardship. Then let's bring that positive energy to ourselves, so that we no longer lack what was withheld. If we were abandoned, we take the time to become a faithful companion to ourselves. If we were criticized, we start acknowledging all the things we do right, instead of looking for what we do wrong. We give to ourselves from the fullness of Source what no one else can ever give us, and what no one can ever take away.

Let's look at another example, where we still love our partner who betrayed us, and so we want to forgive. We have open and honest conversations, and set good boundaries. We want to make it work, so we look closely to see where we may have been a part of the problem, and we make changes. In some cases, this means that the relationship is placed on a new foundation; both people grow enough for things to work out.

Other times, it may work for a while but again we are betrayed. Taking responsibility for our role, we see we have grown, while the other person hasn't. We cannot allow disrespect of our values and boundaries, so we must go our own way without our partner. It's now possible to make the break without any resentment or ill feelings, setting our partner free of any obligation, knowing that true love has nothing to do with sharing the same space. It's only the ego that feels hurt and wants to lash out in some way, overtly or covertly. By walking away from the relationship, we honor both ourselves and our partner, as expressions of one God, each with the ability to choose our actions. We have begun to see through the eyes of God: We are all loved by God unconditionally.

The part of us that wants to keep blaming is like a four-year-old who got punished and never had a chance to express any feelings, to feel and heal them. When we have the desire to attack and blame, that is the hurt little four-year-old inside. But we don't kick this child, slap the kid, or punish again. A four-year-old doesn't know any better.

So be kind to yourself. Be gentle. We just need to hold and love that hurting part of us. It deserves to be felt and to be heard, exactly as it is.

Throughout this book I will assist in moving you up the mental, emotional, and spiritual scale to recognize that there are higher realities. As you discover them you become free of the lower ones—the material world. You may not be there yet, and that's alright, because we have only just started on this journey on the path towards getting free of the pain, to becoming fully empowered again.

The good news is, happiness is our true nature; it's already within us, even if it's temporarily hidden under the unhappiness of unforgiveness. Many of us are unhappy—for different reasons. It's interesting to notice that the reasons why we are unhappy are precisely the reasons why other people are happy. We are unhappy because we are in a relationship; other people are unhappy because they don't have a relationship. When we consciously withdraw blame from anything as the cause of our unhappiness, we allow it to appear at its highest potential—as it is, without judgment. As long as we attach a cause to unhappiness, we are guaranteed to keep that feeling; but when there is no cause for it, it can dissolve, and then what will naturally arise within us is happiness, because that is our true nature.

Really think about this: When there is no cause for unhappiness, happiness arises within you. The only reason you don't feel happy is because you have a belief that there is a cause for your unhappiness. Let go of all the reasons—see things as they are, without any judgment—and forgiveness will be automatic.

As a visible expression of a Universal Energy of infinite and eternal good, we can never hurt or diminish or negatively affect that field of energy which is the only permanent Reality there is—what we call Source. Every visible impermanent reality that surrounds us is just a relative projection of the infinite perfection of Source. The original creation is infinite, absolute, perfect, and unchanging, while how we actually see it—through the filters of our egoic perception—is finite, relative, imperfect, and forever changing. We've been given the free will to do whatever we want in this relative realm of projection. We can act contrary to the qualities inherent in Source, but that only affects the visible world. We then experience the consequences of our thoughts, beliefs, and actions in our human bodies, and affairs. Our actual, spiritual body always remains whole, complete and perfect, without blemish.

SHADOWS OF FORGIVING

Shadows are a core reason why we don't forgive. It's important to understand, however, that in and of themselves, shadows are not bad. They are divine qualities, but when they're *judged*, they show up as destructive versions of themselves—when for instance, *selfish* becomes destructive. When a quality is embraced and integrated, then it's still the negative polarity, but with its positive result: We call it *self-care*.

WHY FORGIVENESS WORKS AND WHY IT DOESN'T

The reason a quality is coming out destructively is because of an early experience, where the result of doing something was painful, and maybe we were even punished for it. When it comes to polarity, negative doesn't mean bad; it means opposite and necessary. For instance, gender has a polarity—the feminine being the negative polarity and the masculine the positive one. That doesn't mean women are bad and men are good. It's just a polarity.

We need to integrate our shadows. We can reach forgiveness through healing shadows; but first, we must understand what they really are.

When we are born, we come into this world endowed with all the attributes and aspects of our Source, which are spiritually whole, complete, and perfect. As we grow, we have experiences—some good and some bad. We have likes and dislikes. We reject the aspects that had painful consequences for us; we judge them "bad" and unwanted in this three-dimensional world, which has laid down certain rules of appropriate behavior. We also create our own rules for what we want or don't want.

For example, when we were little, and rushed around the house screaming with joy at finally running without falling flat on our face, maybe we got reprimanded. We were told to be more careful, not to make so much noise; and suddenly we felt deflated, unappreciated. The way we expressed joy was improper, maybe even punished, and so expressing our feelings became bad. Maybe we insistently demanded a cookie or ice cream when mom was cooking dinner, and she said *No, stop bothering me! Can't you see I'm busy?* With that, we got the message that asking for what we want is not acceptable. However, when we helped mom with her chores, then we got a cookie!

In our experience, perhaps daydreaming was called being *lazy*, wanting a cookie was being *demanding*, trying something new that didn't work was being *stupid*, and not sharing our toys became *selfish*. Painful consequences followed, so we didn't want to be like that. From the beginning, we continued to have experiences that either got us punished or rewarded. Some aspects we rejected as "bad" (even though, in truth, every aspect is a part of Source energy and therefore good). We then created a map of reality allowing for a more comfortable life, because we felt that we were on our own, not loved or supported, or not even safe. We had to look after ourselves, become independent, and self-sufficient. There were certain wonderful skills, abilities, and qualities we developed to survive and thrive in that map of reality, all the aspects of us that were necessary, and a blessing on the beginning part of our journey. We managed to take care of ourselves and make our way in the world.

But the problem was, our early map was not spiritually true. Our real purpose was for us to prove that life is supportive, that we are totally loved and taken care of. Our soul is guiding us every step of the way. We could see this, if we would only trust. Remember that everything is set up to help us remember that we are the expression of Spirit, simply having a human experience. That means there are no bad aspects of us, since they are all expressions of Source energy. As long as we judge and reject them, we will experience them according to our belief. What's more, we can only operate at half our capacity, because the soul has given us 100 percent of everything needed in life; but we have decided to discard a good percentage of that, considering it "bad." Our life, which worked well for a certain length of time, now starts to fall apart. Things don't work as well as they used to, because we're living in a consciousness too small for who we really are: infinite Spirit.

Now starts the second leg of our journey, where we are asked to find a different perception of life—a more spiritual one—because that is Truth. We must create a new map based on ultimate Truth, not on human experiences. Every aspect we don't like is a shadow, a misperception of our true nature.

Feelings that we're unworthy, incapable, stupid, or greedy, were incorrect perceptions that now need to be reintegrated as valuable partners, so that they will stop sabotaging our life. Spirit is infinitely worthy, capable, intelligent, and generous. The shadow work is seeing how those aspects we experienced as painful have really been helping us all along, in order to develop their opposite polarity—the aspects we, and others, most appreciate about ourselves. When we truly accept shadows as our friends and partners, not enemies, we become grateful for the gifts they have already given us and can now bring to us again.

When we see others as arrogant, lazy, crooks, or liars, it simply means we resonate with that frequency. These qualities are our shadows. Painful experiences in the past have made us reject them, but that doesn't make them disappear; they are just suppressed, locked out of sight. Yet they are still there, sabotaging our success.

Whatever we do surreptitiously, not wanting to be seen—such as when we take some food at our workplace when we know we aren't supposed to—shows us a shadow. Maybe our self-talk is what we would never say to anyone else. That's aggressiveness towards ourselves—even if we think we're not an aggressive person. It could also be that it's a quality we have a very strong judgment about—so it's showing us where we need to become more compassionate and less judgmental.

The shadows of the narrow-minded, judgmental, and racist are often found in heart-centered, spiritual people who reject those qualities as something they know they shouldn't be feeling, since they assume that they have a higher, more expanded consciousness. As I've mentioned, this is called a *spiritual bypass*.

A shadow quality has the same energy as its opposite polarity. *Honest* and *dishonest* are one energy that we see as split into positive and negative aspects in our dualistic world. The first Creation—the spiritual world—is only oneness, wholeness, perfection. Being one, it cannot be divided into parts, which is what we have done in our relative world—giving them different names, like *harmony/discord, love/fear, abundance/lack, beauty/ugliness*. Only after Eve ate of the proverbial apple did humanity fall into duality—separation—where the original perfection was divided into parts and placed on a spectrum of good to bad, right to left, hot to cold, and good to evil.

We seem to live in a three-dimensional world in the realm of duality, yet we are actually in the realm of Oneness. Thus our work is to reconcile those seeming opposites into wholeness—the viewpoint of Spirit. We access Spirit's view through understanding why we have judged some qualities, and how they have been serving us even when we were rejecting them. When we gain an understanding of their value, we give them their rightful place as the divine qualities they really are.

Here is an exercise to help you integrate your shadows.

Shadow Exercise

Once you have identified a shadow—that is, a judgment you have about yourself or others, or anything that pushes your buttons, such as labels like *stupid, selfish, unworthy, failure*, etc., it's time to do some inner work.

First of all, create a safe space in your mind to meet with your shadow—a beautiful environment where you like to be. It could be a clearing in a forest, or a beach by the ocean in the shade of palm trees, or a golden temple with sunlight streaming in through windows set with jewels that refract the light with all the colors of the rainbow. Choose an environment that makes you feel peaceful and lighthearted.

Now imagine you are entering an elevator that is up in your head, and you press on the button that says *Heart*, and the elevator starts going down. You hear a ding, the doors open onto your chosen sanctuary and you make your way to your meditation spot. Notice everything about your environment—the colors, the fragrances, the textures, the sounds of birds chirping, or music playing.

Now go sit in your favorite spot, and invite your shadow to come and join you. Maybe it's your selfish self, or your incompetent self. And notice what it looks like—its clothes, its demeanor, its attitude. Is it small, or large? How old does it appear? And as it comes closer, invite it to come and sit.

Now ask:

What happened, early on in my life, that caused me to create you, or to reject you? What was that event? Listen to what it has to say, and see what it is describing. Maybe you just have a feeling or a sensation of what it feels like. Don't judge anything that appears.

Then you ask:

How have you been helping me? How have you been a blessing to me all along? So far, you have been rejecting that part of you, trying to hide it. You've been trying very hard to be its opposite—to become successful, competent, esteemed. You really developed your capabilities as a consequence of feeling incompetent.

Now you are just asking it to tell you all the ways in which it has helped you to become a better person—ways which so far, you have not been able to see. Listen, reflect, and recognize those gifts.

You could also ask:

Why are you appearing to me now? What's your gift in this moment? You might find that in some area of your life you need to gain more knowledge or more insight, or you need to become more open to the needs of your own body, or to the needs of others, etc., and that's why you are again feeling that shadow.

Now comes a very important question:

What do you need from me to feel loved, valued and safe—so that you can take your rightful and healthy place in my life? Notice, you're not trying to change your incompetent self into a competent one; you're not trying to change a loser into a winner, or a sad part into a joyous one. You're asking to know what that part needs from you to feel that it's appreciated and loved just as it is—selfish, incompetent, etc.—so it can take its healthy and constructive place in your life.

Really listen to what it has to say, because it needs some token of your goodwill. It needs your conscious acceptance.

You may not get an answer right away, because that part may not trust you yet, but persevere. Come back and sit with it every day, and eventually something will pop up in your mind that you can actually do. You're guaranteed to get a message—such as *I need to speak to so-and-so, about such-and-such!* Or *Tell him you don't enjoy those kinds of movies!* Or *Relax in a long, hot bath, instead of a quick shower! Take walks in nature! Eat more vegetables! Drink more water!*

Whatever answer you receive, make sure that you actually implement it right now—or if that's not feasible, then at the latest do it tomorrow, so that your shadow

> really understands you are serious about having a better relationship with it.
>
> Now embrace it and thank it for speaking with you and helping you to truly appreciate it. And as you hold it close, feel it getting smaller and lighter, until it merges with your heart, becoming a part of you that is loved and appreciated as much as the so-called "good" parts of you.

An interesting question to ask is *Does forgiveness ever actually fail?* Even at the different levels of forgiveness (which we go into in Chapters 7 to 10), if we're doing it to feel superior so we don't feel the pain, the truth is, at that level it *is* working for us. We're out of pain, and we get some relief, at least for the time being. However, there are potential negative by-products from staying at that level. We always need to move higher.

That is true of anything we attempt to do to improve a situation. Even the Law of Attraction works—until it doesn't any more, when we start to experience the negative by-products of praying and affirming and doing things from a place of separation and attraction. Nevertheless, at least that process stirs in us a search for a deeper truth. At certain times, such as when we're feeling we're the victim and using forgiveness as a control mechanism, or to feel superior—emotionally speaking, that's an upgrade. To go from victim and depression into control and anger is at least higher up on the vibrational scale. Each step serves its purpose, and it is productive not to skip those stages. It's a process we all have to go through, until forgiveness becomes a way of life.

CHAPTER 4

THE FIVE SIGNS OF A NEED TO FORGIVE

> *Forgiveness is the fragrance the violet sheds*
> *on the heel that has crushed it.*
> —Mark Twain

The five most common signs of unforgiveness are:
- Emotional Instability
- Tendency to Blame
- Financial Issues, Especially Debt
- Compulsive Behaviors and Distractions
- Chronic Physical Challenges

Let me be very clear that our issues aren't all necessarily caused by unforgiveness, so there is no need to feel bad about having them. These problems can potentially stem from other reasons. Wherever our issue comes from, it doesn't serve us to blame anyone, least of all ourselves. Having guilt or shame is another thing we will eventually need to forgive. However, when we have completely forgiven everyone and everything—including ourselves—our life *must* and *will* reveal a new level of order, harmony, and abundance. It's never about blaming the victim!

If you recognize one of these five signs in yourself, it might bring up the question of *who* and *what* to forgive. If you're not clear, don't worry; just be aware that we will go deeper into identifying who and what, and in what sequence, in Chapter 5.

In a very real way, every manifestation of pain, lack, limitation, worry, doubt, or fear, is a telltale sign that there is a forgiveness opportunity. This may seem like too much to comprehend right now, but by the time you're done reading this book you'll understand why. For now, we will focus on the most common and chronic signs that appear.

Any kind of negative feedback or judgment—either of yourself or someone else—is a sure sign of unforgiveness. This includes feeling depressed, easily moved to anger, blaming people or circumstances, fighting with your partner, and resenting your boss or colleagues. In this case, a part of us tends to shut down. We feel constricted, weighed down, almost as if something were preventing our expansion into a vast sphere of possibilities that are just beyond our reach. We wonder: *Why am I always broke? Why do I carry so much debt? Why does my body have one problem after another?* Maybe we're a complainer, and nothing ever seems to work out as we want it to. Perhaps we see problems or bad people everywhere. *If only this would happen—or if that person would change—then I would be happy!*

If we've looked at our life and can't find anyone we need to forgive—we have no grudge or resentment towards anyone, and we've done all the right moves, but things are still not working—then it's time to break down what, specifically, we are struggling with the most. Where do we most want improvement? We might find that we are feeling inadequate, never good enough. When we think others are judging us, that in itself is a negative thought about others—whether it's actually true or not. It's unlikely we have unconditional acceptance, let alone love, towards everyone we know or have known. When you can radiate forgiveness and understanding to everyone and everything indiscriminately and sincerely, you will start resolving every issue, and you will be a person with a truly compassionate heart.

You probably know people who always find fault with whatever appears in their reality. When it rains, they can't go out; when it's sunny, it burns their skin; their partner or spouse is never on time; their favorite dish is either too hot or too cold. For people like this, nothing is ever as they want it, and the continual dissatisfaction impacts their health, their relationships, and their finances. All of life seems to be against them. But really, aren't *they* against *life*? They don't even realize it.

When we're against anything, we are blaming, and not being allowing or forgiving.

The energy of debt is the energy of owing—whether we owe something, or someone owes us—either money, an apology, or redress for some offense. The energy of debt very often translates into financial debt, because we are basically withholding—not giving—something. It could be love, compassion, forgiveness, joy, or money. When we are not *for*-giving, we are *for*-withholding—from another or from our self. When we are willing to release others from their debt—in other words, to forgive them—we are also released from our debts; then abundance can flow into our life again.

When we truly know we have everything already within us, how could anyone owe us anything? It's impossible! No one can give us anything, because in Source we already have it all, spiritually. No one can take anything real away from us, because we can generate whatever we need from this Spirit within us. When we reach the highest level of forgiveness, we will truly understand this fact. Then there can no longer be financial debt manifesting in our life.

Getting angry at the slightest thing that stands in our way demonstrates a lack of acceptance of life, of what is. In essence, that's unforgiveness. Anger fosters heart disease, diabetes, or depression—among many other conditions—as documented by medical research. On the other hand, studies have shown that forgiveness calms stress levels, and improves blood pressure and immune responses. It's so important to forgive, for our own happiness and spiritual growth. When we hold on to pain, resentment, and anger, these emotions harm *us*, not the offender. When feelings traced back to our early childhood repeat themselves in our intimate relationships, it's the core wound of the child that needs healing first. The first step to take is to understand and forgive our parents, which will lead to a better understanding of the present situation and to finding the appropriate solutions.

> *Many of our health challenges are caused by unforgiveness issues, amply demonstrated by both energy healing and medical research. I once had a client who came to me with painful hands covered with angry-looking red blotches. Nothing her doctor prescribed helped in any way. What came up for her was an unforgiveness issue, but she was adamant that there was no one she resented or held a grudge against. I encouraged her to search deeper, asking if there was anything painful that had happened in the last few years. Then she remembered that her dog got run over by a car. Instantly I knew that this was her issue. But she still wasn't aware of being angry or resentful. However, after she consciously worked on forgiving that driver, her condition started improving, and it was completely resolved within a few weeks.*

So often, issues like this are on a subconscious level. So how can we heal if we're not even aware of the feeling?

Life is good, but our life experience is what we make it—through our judgments, actions, and perceptions. What we are feeling today was often not caused by the external circumstance we're blaming. It was already in us from the past, but now it's coming up because it's ready to be released and cleared from our energy field. Sometimes a person or circumstance arises just to make us aware of what was in us that needed to be released—feelings that could not have been expressed when we were younger. When we do the work and reach a higher awareness, it's finally safe to feel and transform these feelings, and that's why they've risen to the surface.

Blaming people or circumstances is a convenient way of not taking proper responsibility for our feelings. Let's not do that any longer. Instead, let's cultivate a mindset that no one is to be blamed for anything. What if everything was no one's fault? Feel how liberating that statement feels: *Everything is no one's fault*! That's the frequency of consciousness that automatically forgives—and also eliminates any further need for forgiveness.

The inherent truth about forgiveness is that ultimately, it really makes our life what we want it to be, because we are expressing two of the core principles upon which all of Life rests: unconditional love and allowance. Where there is love, there cannot be hate or fear. Where there is allowance, there cannot be rejection. Divinity provides unconditional love and allowance. Even in situations that seem chaotic on the surface, if we step back far enough, we'll perceive a higher order of things emerging, and see as the Divine sees.

HOW TO FIND PLACES OF UNFORGIVENESS

The need for forgiveness isn't always obvious, but if we're willing to look, we'll uncover clues. Introspection is always necessary when struggling with any aspect of life. If we're feeling reactive or overwhelmed, it helps to identify in what area of life those feelings arise—health, work, family relationships, or finances. Then we need to ask *What is the story I have going on there? What am I telling myself? What am I believing about myself?* The answers give us important information. Begin journaling about it to understand how it relates to the challenge you are now experiencing.

The consciousness behind our actions is what determines our experience. If the focus is on punishing others, the resulting experience will be bad; if our focus is on simply stopping harm, with a feeling of compassion and allowance for the offender, the experience will be one that feels clean and ethical. For every area of life, we have created certain set points that will not necessarily hold true for another area. For instance, we might feel capable and confident about our work; but when it comes to relationships, we feel incapable of attracting the ideal partner. We may have a strong self-image—never getting ill, eating whatever we want and staying slim—while someone else may eat all the right foods, but still end up getting sick often.

The real principle of life is that consciousness is the cause of our reality. It's the self-image we hold that determines the results we get. If aggressive and selfish people believe they are worthy and capable of being wealthy, they will become rich. A kind and generous person who doesn't feel worthy or abundant will remain poor. The Source of all Life (God) is in everyone and everything, so when we see less than the perfection of God anywhere, we are denying a principle—looking only at a surface appearance, which has been humanly created. We have been told by the Scriptures, "Judge not by appearances" (John 7:24). Forgiveness happens through our willingness to expand our awareness beyond what the physical self perceives, to see from a spiritual standpoint.

Your job as a conscious being is to view every behavior as either love, or a call for love. If people do anything unloving, it means they have forgotten who they really are. If you can remain aware of the spiritual Reality, then they can be reminded of it, too. Would you rather be right, or be happy? You can go on and on about how terrible someone is—and what's more, you may get many other people to agree with you, and even sympathize with you. Or, you could choose to remind others of their spiritual perfection, through your example. When others observe your equanimity, they might just see that there is a better way to live their lives.

Emotional Instability

Let's take a closer look at emotional make-up, and the many aspects of this category. It could be that we easily get upset or triggered; if we are hasty to react, that's a typical sign. Perhaps we hate our job and when we get home, the slightest excuse is a good enough reason to pick a fight with our spouse—something we wouldn't dare do at work. Maybe we feel insecure, and not appreciated.

Say you have been in your job for a while now, you would really like a promotion, and you actually apply for it. But when it comes to having that interview, you suddenly feel insecure, and don't know whether you can handle it. Excuses come up. It will require a bigger time commitment; you're afraid of being a disappointment to yourself and to the company; you feel unworthy. These feelings come up every time there is a chance to progress. So you sabotage yourself.

This time, you really search your memory for the point where those feelings started, because you know you have all the skills necessary for this promotion. Maybe you remember that as a teenager, you once failed to keep an appointment with a friend. At the last minute a better option came up, and you phoned to say you couldn't come. The friend was really angry because she counted on you and even missed going to a movie with her family. You felt really bad, untrustworthy, unreliable, incapable of keeping your word. In this case, it's time to see that you are no longer that teenager; you need to forgive yourself for past mistakes so your life can move forward.

When we find ourselves emotionally reactive to a situation or person—feeling angry, powerless, and lashing out, then we have a judgment, and we are in human consciousness. We have cut ourselves off from Source, which never judges anything. We have joined people in the exact same wrong behavior we are accusing them of. That's living a lie, which automatically separates us from the Divine, blocking Its infinite supply of good.

In spiritual consciousness, there is no destructive quality, and so righteous anger equates with power. We can use it with integrity to correct a situation, and still be in a powerful sense of the Self—where our personality (ego) doesn't feel attacked or diminished. We feel no hatred or resentment, so we have full control of our expression of anger. In this scenario, a situation can be righted, and it won't degenerate. There is an example of this in the Scriptures, when Jesus chased the money-lenders out of the temple (see Matthew 21:12–13); he overturned the tables where they were conducting their business, and they could easily have overpowered him. It was his higher consciousness, rooted in Divinity, that did not allow them to retaliate; instead they had to pay attention.

Tendency to Blame

When we attack—verbally or physically—or when we even have just a *desire* to attack anyone—including ourselves—it's because we hold blame for what was done, or for what happened; or we beat ourselves up. The desire to lash out in anger is a typical reaction when we have been hurt in some way, or when we experience fear.

For example, a child runs out into the street right under the wheels of your car. The fear you had of hitting that youngster can be so great that you jump out, grab the kid and shout *Never do that again! You hear me?* But that's not actually having full control over yourself.

If someone has been poking you with a stick, and asking that person to stop doesn't work, simply forgiving and doing nothing about it is being a doormat. You are not standing in your power, or respecting yourself as an expression of the Divine. There is an obvious call to action there to do something so that the painful situation does not continue. But this can be done without destructive anger or a desire to retaliate.

When there is any kind of self-sabotage, there may be unconscious blame. So often, when we don't go for what we want, it's because of a subconscious memory of something that happened when we were little. Perhaps we demanded what we wanted and got punished for it.

Another aspect that can surface is the need to forgive ourselves when we have harmed someone else. Hopefully, we would never willingly cause harm to anyone, but sometimes an accident happens. If we hit a cyclist who suddenly came from a side road at night, and landed the rider in hospital, we feel remorse. We're genuinely sorry. To forgive ourselves, we take full responsibility—both for the harm caused to the other person, and also for the hurt we're inflicting on ourselves due to feeling so bad about what we've done.

Financial Issues, Especially Debt

There are countless aspects to financial issues. It may seem like we can make money, and yet it appears to melt away as fast as it comes. It's then important to look back at your childhood for deeper issues. Maybe when you were given some money for your birthday, and you rushed off to buy a huge bag of candy, your mom got upset. *Look at you, wasting money, when you could have saved it to buy that toy you really wanted! You can't be trusted to manage money!* Perhaps such a moment made you feel like you could never have enough for everything you wanted, or that you were incapable of wisely choosing. That belief is playing out now, in your adult life. Forgiving your mom—who was only doing the best she could with what she knew—would free you of those limiting beliefs, and soon, your finances would improve.

Maybe you're struggling with earning enough to make ends meet, and you remember an experience when you were a child that made you feel like you were a failure at managing money. Perhaps you got a message that girls weren't good with money. In that case, you first need to forgive yourself for thinking that you're somehow deficient; and you'll also need to forgive those who gave you that idea in the first place.

Maybe somewhere in the past you made a mistake, and because of it either you or your family suffered financial loss; this would make you not trust yourself around money. The result would be that you shrunk your world where money was concerned, so you wouldn't do that again. And now you live in that small, protective area where you don't have much money; nor do you have much opportunity, because there is unforgiveness. When you forgive yourself for that mistake—and gain an understanding of the lessons and the blessings—you will be able to let go of those shadows of *irresponsible* or *stupid*, and become more open to trusting yourself as a channel for greater abundance to flow through you.

In addition to doing the inner work towards forgiveness, you can create a mantra. Repeating a phrase throughout the day helps you anchor an idea in consciousness. Choose something positive such as *I have unlimited abundance and I am capable of managing it!* or *My monthly income always easily exceeds my expenses.*

When we have financial debt, we need to find where we are holding others in energetic debt. Where do we give our time, energy, or supply to someone with the expectation of a future gain? An example would be paying for a college education for someone, such as your children, and expecting gratitude, or hoping to be supported later. Does the sun shine its life-giving rays, hoping for a gift in return? Does God give us life and the whole Earth as a playground, demanding something for Itself? Sometimes we see parents saying to their children *Look at all I did for you; now it's your turn to look after me*. That attitude holds people in energetic debt, and that's why they may actually be in financial debt.

Let's release all expectations of getting anything back. We may have been a channel of abundance for others, but they are not our Source. The Source of all well-being has been blocked by our choosing to view a person or a thing as our Source. In the Scriptures, the First Commandment from God is, "Thou shalt have no other gods before Me" (Exodus 20:3). When we know that there is truly only One Source, then divine energy can flow to us again. And it will come through some physical channel—whether from our children, an inheritance, or winning the lottery.

Compulsive Behaviors and Distractions

When the memory of what has been done to us is so painful that we're unwilling to look at it, talk about it, or even have anyone else know about it, it can turn into an addiction. We think it makes us look bad, weak, helpless, or stupid. We feel ashamed. That's often the case when there has been abuse, whether verbal or physical. Either we feel ashamed of our role in it, and we need to forgive ourselves; or we didn't do what we could have done to help someone; or we joined a group that was banding together against someone, verbally or otherwise. Or, we might be ashamed that such a thing could have been done to us. As a reaction we may become self-centered, and cultivate a false sense of self-esteem and importance—an arrogance that will never serve us in the long run. If we see ourselves as inconsequential, insignificant, or worthless, these are all shadows we need to integrate.

It could be that when you were eight, you joined a group of school kids who were all laughing at a student who was different. Even now, as you remember it, you think *How could I have done that?* The memory comes up only so that you can really look at it, and forgive yourself.

There may be a long-standing, unresolved situation that is still alive and painful, and we don't want to be reminded of it. Perhaps we have not forgiven some aspect of it, or we're afraid of being judged for our role in it. Doing forgiveness work on what's both known and unknown, both conscious and unconscious, will help resolve it.

Maybe what has been done to someone we love seems unforgivable, but we still intellectually know we need to forgive. We don't want to look at our own feelings of vindictiveness and hate, or allow others (especially our significant other) to know about these feelings, so we compensate with distractions—like food or shopping—and close off a whole part of us from life. We can't be fully honest, fully authentic, because we're ignoring a part of ourselves. Become conscious of what is behind the addictions and distractions, and you'll be able to forgive.

Chronic Physical Challenges

It would seem that there can be no link between forgiveness and problems with the physical body, but that is just not true. Since psychiatry and psychology have become interested in the impact of forgiveness upon physical health, it has now become common knowledge that stress is bad for our health, and that forgiveness allows us to let go of the chronic stressors that are a burden on our system.

It's impossible to point to any one particular physical issue and say that generally, it comes from unforgiveness, because we are all unique individuals with different life experiences, different propensities, and different habits of thought. The physical problem could be any ailment—from arthritis to heart trouble, to the case of the disfiguring skin blotches I mentioned earlier.

Whatever issue we have, if it has not been helped by the usual medical treatments, then this is more often than not an indication that the cause is in the emotional, mental, spiritual, or dimensional realms. In such a case, in order for the symptoms to release, we need to learn something significant for our personal evolution.

In addition, we all have a life mission, which may require that our condition does not shift—or not yet—so that a higher good may emerge from it, of which we are presently unaware. Life is complex, and our perspective is very limited; there are multiple reasons for every circumstance. Our unconditional loving stance, with acceptance that everything happens only for our highest good, is the best attitude to adopt. This positive attitude will generate gratitude, which will allow us to have the best experience possible even in the midst of suffering through the condition. Once that loving outlook is firmly anchored, only then should we turn to what else can be physically done to improve a condition.

There was once a woman in constant pain whose body was gradually becoming crippled. She had been going to doctors for years, but nobody could help her. As a last resort, she went to an energy healer, and after some conversation about her life experiences, the

THE FIVE SIGNS OF A NEED TO FORGIVE

healer had a moment of insight and said *You told me about this incident with those two men. Have you forgiven them for that?* The woman's whole face changed as she retorted *I will never forgive them for that!* Her unforgiveness was the real reason for all her issues. She left, full of hate and resentment. That was the end of the session; we don't know whether she thought about what the healer revealed to her. We don't know if she ever tried to apply the treatment of forgiveness. If holding on to anger, hatred, and resentment can have such a devastating effect, wouldn't it be worth her while to at least give forgiveness a chance?

CHAPTER 5

WHO AND WHAT TO FORGIVE

Alice's story:

It was pitch black and pouring rain as I drove myself and my two boys away from the nightmare we had been living. Afraid of what he would do when he found us missing, I called to tell him we had left. He begged me to stop, to tell him where I was so he could get us. I didn't. I dialed my parents. My dad gave me simple instructions, kept me driving and talked me the rest of the way in, while I had only a vague awareness of where we were.

When we arrived at the shelter, the hosts led us to a small room. The boys sat on the floor and played while I answered questions and filled out registration forms. The rules were strict: set curfew; set bedtime; children could not be left unattended; daily chores; no visitors. Then we were shown our room. It had a single bed and a bunk bed. We woke in the morning and went for a walk. With the first step outside the door, I knew we were home. I knew God had brought us home.

The other day I came across the admissions folder for that shelter where we stayed that first night. Inside was the picture that my older son had drawn while waiting for me to register. On that dark, sad, raining night, he had drawn a picture of a bright sunshiny day. That is how it felt to be finally free from the prison of abuse.

During our ten-year marriage, I conceded and simply accepted the abuse. But with acceptance I was still imprisoned. Now that I have broken free of that prison, I can choose to forgive my former husband's actions, but I no longer choose to accept them. With forgiveness I feel no more anger. Forgiveness allows me greater perspective and helps me see our relationship for what it was.

I know I will still struggle. But if I were not to forgive him, I could not objectively guide my boys through the complications that come with our divorce. They understand on some level why I left their father, but they will also still love him. Forgiveness allows me to tell my boys stories of the good times, memories that show them that they come from a place of love.

Most of all, I work on forgiving myself. I have long since let go of the idea that I was at fault for the abuse in my marriage. However, I still feel the tremendous weight of the effect this has had on my boys. A mother should protect her children. I failed them. I allowed them to see things no child should ever see. That is not something I can make go away. It happened, and every day we deal with its lasting effects.

FORGIVING ANOTHER, FORGIVING YOURSELF

Our core wounds are often the forgotten place that needs forgiveness. For instance, let's say that when you were five years old, you came home from school, proud of having learned a new song. You jumped up and down on the sofa, singing as loud as you could, thinking you would impress Mom. But instead, she responded *Don't make so much noise! Your father is working! And stop jumping like that; the sofa is not a trampoline!* You stopped, feeling totally rejected and misunderstood, thinking *Nobody appreciates me. No one likes my new song.*

That's a core wound for a five-year old, which a child doesn't know how to resolve right then, which will be triggered every time anything similar happens—such as a teacher saying your essay didn't follow the assignment; a classmate seeming to ignore you; a friend not responding to your enthusiastic greeting as you hoped; your partner neglecting you; and so on.

In this scenario, now as an adult you have your mind set on taking an exotic holiday in Hawaii, but your spouse says *It's way too expensive; why don't we just relax closer to home, in the mountains or on the beach? We have everything we need right on our doorstep!* You get upset and angry, and you think *My desires don't seem to matter. Money is more important than I am. Am I even loved at all?* Notice the escalation in the chain of thought—out of proportion with the mere fact of deciding where to go for a holiday. At this point in time, of course you don't even remember that instance when you were five, jumping around and singing a new song.

All those levels will have to be forgiven. This time, you can also forgive your partner for not considering your desires. But the next time anything happens, you will be triggered again, because the core wound of the five-year old is still there, smoldering. Making the effort to identify the earliest wound is well worthwhile, because you will finally see the occurrence with an adult's mind, for what it really was. It was not rejection and lack of love—because your mom dearly loved you—it was just a misunderstanding of the facts. Now, when you heal that wound, all the other, smaller triggers can unravel on their own. You'll have a greater awareness of what is really happening in your present life and you will no longer be triggered by inconsequential things.

We often don't fully realize that many of the issues and challenges we are experiencing—and earnestly trying to solve by some specific process that relates to the symptoms we have—are really by-products of a story of unforgiveness from long ago. The incidents are buried so deep that we've forgotten about them. Or, they are still on the surface because they are so painful, and we can't forget, so we're constantly repressing them every time they come to mind, and we don't forgive. Typically, 90 percent of reactions are from past unforgiven incidents, and only 10 percent come from the present one. When the past is cleaned up, the actual issue can be addressed in the moment, and quickly resolved.

Whenever our partner is in the mix, maybe we have done enough work on ourselves, and become more loving and allowing; however, where that obnoxious person in the office is concerned, we are still in ego and self-righteousness. Our issues aren't always going to be at the same level in different areas of our life. We might do the work and go up a notch in one situation, but then feel stuck in another. So it's always a good idea to check in and see if there is still a fragment from another area that we didn't really address.

VARIOUS LIFE STRUCTURES IN WHICH TO FORGIVE

Health

Generally speaking, we don't recognize that traumas in childhood have created shadows of feeling unworthy, unloved, not good enough, and so on—and that this is the root cause of our discomfort and inabilities. We were not mature enough then to consciously deal with the feelings that came up when certain events happened. To protect us, the body stored that ball of energy—about the size of an orange—until it was possible for us to safely release it. Over time, the pressure put on the part of the body housing the emotion affects the tissues around it, and that's why we get aches and pains for seemingly no reason. We attribute it to old age, considering it normal. When we learn to release the specific emotions connected to that pain through energy healing, the discomfort can gradually lessen, and sometimes even miraculously disappear.

Experiences early on in life can have a considerable influence on how we think of ourselves, or react to circumstances as an adult. Say, for example, that we are often unwell, and because of that we miss out on many activities that we would have enjoyed. Friends feel sorry for us and come to visit, so that is our pay-off. Maybe we are also afraid to say *no* to anyone, and so we end up saying *yes* to others, when really, we wanted to say *no*. We become afraid of losing friends, of not being part of a group. This could be a coping mechanism we developed as a child when we didn't want to go to school, so we pretended to be sick, and our parents didn't see through it, and let us stay home. We did it again, realizing it was an easy way to get out of chores, and pretty soon we became a sickly child. Just the *idea* of going to gym practice—or of anything we didn't want to do—actually made us catch a cold, or the flu, or laryngitis.

As adults, we begin to realize what we really want, yet we're still sickly, and that makes us unable to participate in activities we like, so eventually we investigate to find out why this is. We soon discover the pattern of not wanting to upset others; and when we resist anything, it ends up in sickness. That's the clarity needed to regain full health, but it requires courage to reverse our habits. We learn to say *yes* only when we really mean it, and *no* when we really mean no—regardless of what others might think. Then we find out that usually others are quite willing to accept a *no* without question!

Here is where we learn not to blame ourselves. We can't blame our inner child for doing what was comfortable, because that kid didn't know any better. We accept and understand that inner child, and fully love that child within. It's our love that will allow the inner child to become a helpful team-mate to the adult we are.

Having a negative self-concept about our body can be sabotaging our life. I know a woman who thought she was ugly, and couldn't even look at herself in the mirror. She mentioned once that her parents were forever saying how beautiful her little sister was, but they never said anything nice about her—so she assumed she was ugly. In fact, there was nothing wrong with her face at all. She started the work of forgiving her parents for being unthinking and unaware of the harm they were causing. She brought up all the feelings of being less than her sister, unloved, and unappreciated; she saw that these feelings were a child's interpretation of the actual facts. She gave herself permission to detail her face in the mirror and see that it was a perfectly normal face, with a very fine bone structure. She could finally go out on dates without that crippling feeling of being ugly.

Abuse is another aspect that impacts almost all of us in one way or another, whether it's emotional, mental, or physical. It leads to us feeling judged or rejected—whether for being fat or skinny, not good at sports, not good with figures, or feeling we're a burden. That's always a journey of recognizing the spiritual truth: that we are an individual expression of Source energy, and nothing can be either added or taken away from who we truly are. The abuse has possibly caused us to turn towards spirituality, and so it has served its purpose; now we can let the judgment go and forgive those who were simply instruments for that shift towards a higher understanding to occur.

Wealth

If we never seem to make enough to cover our expenses, or we earn money, but it seems to disappear as fast as it came in, then maybe we've had a childhood experience where our father scolded us for losing our allowance, or for spending it on trivialities—and he said if we keep doing that, we'll never have enough. But those were things we really wanted as a kid. And so we became constricted around money, became conscious of spending it till it's gone, rather than circulating it so it could bring us lasting benefits. Perhaps we were told we were not good at managing money; or that girls were not good around money; or we heard our parents talk disparagingly about those people who spend all their money on the latest fashion trends and then don't have enough to pay bills.

Closely look at your beliefs around money, and where they came from. Were you taught to save money? Were you told *Money doesn't grow on trees*? Were you taught that money is scarce? Did you learn that you have to work hard to get it? Now ask yourself if these ideas are true, or just beliefs that can be changed for a more empowering view.

Do you have feelings of not wanting someone else to succeed? These vengeful feelings are destructive; they block us from achieving what we want. The truth is, what you give to another, you ultimately give to yourself; what you withhold from another you also withhold from yourself. Because spiritually, we are all One.

Another block is when we believe we don't deserve to succeed, or to have what we want. This shows a lack of self-worth, a habit of comparing ourselves to others who succeed. Essentially, we're living the lie that we are not supported by God.

Knowing that the Universe is always supportive is a first step. Knowing what we want, and deciding to go for it, is already half the battle. Then we look at how to co-create the circumstances that match our desire. We have to start to really do something towards our goal, which will increase our self-esteem and self-worth, which in turn will manifest as success and abundance.

Energetically, we raise our self-worth through practicing gratitude. Thankfulness is an acknowledgment that a gift has been given. Anchoring gratitude every day—multiple times a day—increases our self-worth and establishes a higher vibrational frequency. There is always something to be grateful for—the sunshine, the rain, a comfortable bed—thus your vibration rises again. Incrementally, you start believing you can succeed.

Work and Creativity

What if we have issues with our boss or colleagues at work? We feel that they disregard, criticize, and don't value us. What is the cause of our experience? A principle of life is that nothing can come into our experience except through an activity of our consciousness. Maybe early on we felt disregarded, unwanted, or criticized, and now we're projecting that onto others. Perhaps we heard our parents say that their boss never appreciated them, or that their colleagues were self-seeking or mean; and now, that expectation has become your default. We may have already played that out in school and in college. The people who gave us those ideas had no intention of doing harm; they were unaware of the impact that it would have, and what kind of a map of life their child would create because of those ideas. We need to forgive them, and then forgive ourselves, for accepting those concepts back then without question.

Sometimes when we have a pattern of not following through and completing projects—such as losing weight, writing a book, or starting a business—what is the pain associated with completing that project? There are two motivations for any action: either seeking pleasure, or avoiding pain. It may be that the project is too hard—we think we won't succeed and then we'll feel incapable—so we give up on it. Examine where else in life we easily give up on the things we really want. Where are we not keeping our word—either a promise to ourselves or to another person? How are we being self-indulgent? All those instances need forgiveness. The clarity gained will contribute to making us better equipped not to yield to seeking mere comfort and convenience, but to succeed.

If you are the type of person who says you wish you could draw, or paint—but you say *I can't even draw a stick-figure*—that's an exaggeration, and not even true. Everyone can draw a stick figure. But what may have happened in an art class in fourth grade, is that the teacher looked at your work and said *What's that supposed to be? Even the colors are wrong*! and you were crushed, so you never opened up again to the creative part of you that saw things differently.

Maybe you wanted to play an instrument, but were told you should study something that will provide a good steady income—like business, or engineering. With music, only the best succeed, so you decided that you're not all that good. Maybe your parents said *I won't always be there to support you*! We listened to "the voice of reason," and studied marketing instead. Nowadays you have a job and an income, but there is no happiness or sense of achievement in life, because what your soul yearns for is music rather than selling products. That lack of joy and deep dissatisfaction will start coloring other areas of your life—like health, relationships, and personal development. They'll all start to stagnate, and problems will continue, until you begin giving some expression to your deepest desire. It doesn't mean being foolish and giving up your job to play music; but you can start to play in your free time, getting together with musician friends, giving your talent space, and being open to where it might lead in the future.

Relationships

This is the area where unforgiveness is most obvious. If we have a deep and unrecognized childhood feeling of resentment for our parents, it could have potentially created a cascade of events—both with them and also with other people—which all need forgiving. If our father abandoned the family, we might have felt unworthy of love, and stopped trusting men. We became independent, not relying on anyone, never letting a man fully into our heart because of a fear we will again feel destroyed, like when we were a child.

There are not a lot of different unforgiveness stories. There are really only one or two big ones—at least, big in a child's mind—and the rest of our challenges are just wounding us over and over, unwittingly, in our adult life relationships. Maybe we need to forgive our partner for not being there for us. Perhaps it was only a minor thing, but in our mind, it got amplified by all the other instances from the past of feeling unloved or abandoned. When we realize our reaction to something in the present was excessive, we can take ourselves back to the first time we had that feeling; truly forgive our parents; understand how that event was a blessing because it helped us grow; and then we can see all our relationships in that context.

Spirituality

Say that we were brought up in a certain religion, and we questioned certain things being taught, which were not logical to us; but our parents or others in authority did not listen. *Who are you to think you know better?* That disrespect from authority figures built resentment, so as soon as we could, we abandoned going to church and maybe even started to search for wiser teachings. But nothing we learned was completely satisfying, so we ended up with no religion.

Then we landed a job where we were told what to do, but we thought it would be better to do things another way. Nobody listened, so again we became resentful. We traced our feelings back to their source, and understood how our parents or teachers did the best they knew how; they were just teaching us what had been taught to them. We saw the blessings, and realized how we have grown because of the hardships.

WHO AND WHAT TO FORGIVE

When we fully forgive the mother we love, soon afterwards we'll find that work relationships start to improve all on their own; our suggestions are now listened to, and sometimes even carried out. That's because we are no longer projecting the energy of not being considered or valued that was in our make-up before. That past part of ourselves—feeling unimportant, unworthy, and passed over—is simply no longer there.

Another possible scenario is that our life path has taken us into a spiritual practice that has created tensions with family members, so that we have little or no contact with them. They may be criticizing us because of having renounced their religion for another, so we start resenting them. Forgiveness is needed because their intentions are good, even if they're misguided. Once we have forgiven ourselves for our judgments, and we're anchored in our spirituality, we accept them as they are, not as we think they should be.

When we believe we deserve punishment, that's not a right understanding of spirituality. In the Mind of God there is no such thing as punishment. There is only love and allowance. God sees us all as equally endowed, equally worthy emanations of the Divine. How we choose to express the Divinity we truly are into the visible world of duality where we live is totally our responsibility. Spiritual principles we are often unaware of always operate and override material laws.

One of these spiritual principles is that *consciousness is cause*. It's not so much the actions we take, but the consciousness behind them that determines our experience. That is why sometimes the outcome of a seemingly good deed can be humanly bad, and sometimes an action that is humanly bad can result in good. It is the consciousness of the person acting that determines the outcome. There are of course other reasons too—such as karma, purpose of life, and so on—which are complex. We need to accept the fact that, from our limited perspective, we don't see the complete picture of ultimate perfection that God sees. We don't always know what is best to move us up the spiritual ladder. Often, the most traumatic event is the exact thing that was needed. We see only the obstacles we must overcome on the path towards that ultimate perfection. We don't often realize that every obstacle is there only to teach us something and to move us forward.

FINDING YOUR OWN FORGIVENESS ISSUE TO WORK WITH

By now, you have probably already found a few people or situations that still need forgiveness in your life. When any experience is very highly charged, that will be the one holding the greatest possibility of transformation. If we can trace our feelings back to the earliest time we felt something similar, that will likely be the original event, which has been reinforced time and time again throughout our life until now. We're conscious enough to look at it with an adult's eye now, and ready to heal the original core wound. After the understanding comes, we let ourselves feel all the feelings and let go of all blame for the people involved; then the present issue will resolve itself.

For some people, saying things out loud works best; for others it will be seeing things in their mind's eye. You could take a symbolic action, or even go and talk with the person. The more senses you can enlist concerning the issue, the better chance you'll have of your forgiveness being effective.

When we embark on the forgiveness journey on our own, it has a lot of pitfalls, because unhealed wounds, fears, and doubts will emerge. We may feel out of control, or gain very little clarity about what's really going on, because we're coming up against a lot of mental or emotional blind spots. We all have them, so it's a really good idea to find a guide to take us on that journey. Ask a friend for some external feedback, or ask others who can take the journey with you while doing their own forgiveness work, so you can support each other—a family member you trust, or a qualified therapist, coach, or healer. If no one comes to mind right now, and you would like to have personal help on your forgiveness journey, visit my website www.janiaaebi.com and see what you find there to assist you.

Finally, if we have people in our life where every time we see them or think about them, it triggers an unwanted emotional charge or a judgment, or if we have memories that come back with an energetic charge—even if we have done the inner work on all the levels—it may be because we have unresolved soul contracts. These are agreements we have made with other souls, before ever being born, which are now playing out. This aspect will be discussed in Chapters 8 and 9.

HIERARCHY OF FORGIVENESS

Almost always, we will find some obvious parts of us that need acceptance, love, and forgiveness. Otherwise, we would not have been triggered so much. Those parts have the same epithets we gave that other person: *inconsiderate, unfeeling, selfish, aggressive, controlling,* etc. These are our shadows, which we need to see the value of, to love, and to integrate.

It's helpful to get clear on who or what most needs forgiveness, to determine the optimal sequence of what needs to be forgiven. Is it the current issue, or the original, childhood issue? The one that brings the strongest charge is the one that we need to address first.

Initial core wounds mostly happen in early childhood, up to around the age of seven; they reverberate in the psyche and change the way we see life from then on. Often, healing the original issue will make the whole chain dissolve. But even if it doesn't, it will then be much easier to forgive those subsequent experiences with the understanding of what that core wound really was.

If there is a very strong charge on the present issue, that is the place to start the work. Then, event by event, you can journey back to the core wound and finally heal that. For example, when someone has been really mean and we're triggered, we feel angry and the pain brings back other instances of hurt that we haven't thought about for ages. In that case, that's a signal that we're ready and able to process those old negative feelings. We thought we had forgotten those instances, but they are still lodged inside, and they'll keep coming up to compound the hurt. Over time, all that toxic energy we are storing not only in our memory but in our body, will cause physical discomfort or disease. When we understand that, we can start determining what most needs forgiveness. Maybe the charge around a parent is not so strong anymore, but we do really feel it about our partner—so that's the place to start. Eventually, now that we know the mechanics, we can work our way back.

Maybe you had a date who was late, and while waiting for him you got increasingly upset, feeling *I don't matter*! Then when he appeared, you flew into a rage. If you told a friend about this, your friend might say *Why didn't you just ask him what happened? Maybe he wanted to call or text, and found that his phone was dead, but he got there as quickly as he could*. The whole problem would have been nonexistent for someone who did not have your core wound.

WHO AND WHAT TO FORGIVE

When we decide to no longer blame anyone or anything as the reason for us being hurt or unhappy—not our past lives, not our parents, not the people or situations in our life—forgiveness becomes automatic. There is no one to blame, so there is no one to be forgiven. That is the true essence of forgiveness, and true freedom.

Forgiveness works because we have absolute control over our thoughts and actions. Resolving our feelings can't be done by beating ourselves up into love or peace; that's a contradiction in terms. Our foundation must be that our internal self-talk is gentler and more understanding, not rejecting any parts of us, but making sure we are taking all our flaws with us on the journey—to be slowly transformed into their original perfection by unconditional love. They then release their gifts, to make our life what we want it to be.

CHAPTER 6

THE FOUR LEVELS OF FORGIVENESS

*When you forgive, you in no way change the past—
but you sure do change the future.*
—Bernard Meltzer

Forgiveness is on a spectrum, with four core levels. These levels closely follow the levels of consciousness, so we are always vacillating between them. Over the next several chapters we are going to be speaking about those levels and how to bring this work to bear within them. We want to be able to tell at which level we are, and how to ascend up the ladder to ultimate forgiveness.

In some areas, we may feel more like a victim, and in that case, we need to start at the Victim level. In other areas, we might feel capable and empowered, so we jump to the level of Creator. Depending on what we're forgiving—and the level of consciousness in that particular area—it will be easier or harder to forgive. We have a dual nature, so both sides have to be honored. Forgiveness at the highest level touches the spiritual, which is seeing nothing wrong—that is, seeing with the eyes of God. On the other hand, being human, we need to go through all the levels to get there, and not to skip any, or we will find ourselves stuck; then we'll have to go back to the level where we did not fully forgive, start there, and try again.

You can't learn to ride a motorcycle before learning to ride a bicycle. You can't run before you've learned to walk. The actual crawling stage builds all kinds of connections in the brain that are really necessary and valuable for when we start walking and developing more advanced skills. The same principle holds true with spiritual levels of development. It's smart to start at the first level, and make sure we complete it.

LEVELS OF CONSCIOUSNESS

Our life is basically broken down into four stages of consciousness, and the symptoms we experience are very often tied to our stories of unforgiveness. There are two main areas where we need to forgive: either it's someone else, or some part of ourselves. This can include a group—a tribe, religious affiliation, or nation. Ultimately, because we are One with Spirit, which is expressing *as* each one of us, all forgiveness is self-forgiveness. We are actually not *in* the world, but the whole world is in our consciousness.

The levels of consciousness are:
1. Victim
2. Creator/Manifestor
3. Channel/Conduit
4. Union/Oneness

We progressively move through these stages, but they are not linear. We can go in and out of them in a day, depending on our circumstances. We can also be at different levels in different life structures. For example, we feel in control and powerful in the work place, but unsure and powerless in our romantic relationship. We can be in Level 1 in one area, Level 2 in another, and Level 3 in another. Since we're still human in form, we can always revert back into any of the previous stages. Even if we do fall back, once a higher stage has been reached, it is easier to climb back to a level we've already attained, because some of the stuff has been cleared.

1. **Victim Level**

    When we start off in life, things are done for us; we have no power, no responsibility. At about the age of two, the ego is being born and we try to assert our will over others. Forgiveness has no meaning as yet—we want what we want, and we want it now—but more and more often, we might not get it, so Victim consciousness starts.

    As we get older, we are told not to hold grudges. We perceive being hurt, but we are told our younger siblings don't yet understand, and we should know better! So we may start feeling superior, and our sense of power gets reinforced. Yet in many ways, we are still victims of our parents, teachers, and adults in general. We look to others to do things for us, to save us from the consequences of our actions. In many ways, that's comfortable, but it's also very limiting. We start rebelling against authority, with painful results. Taking responsibility and claiming our power will loosen this disempowered sense of self and raise us to the next level of consciousness.

2. **Creator/Manifestor Level**

    Here, we come into an empowered sense of self, with no one dictating to us. We live in that consciousness most of our lives, believing we have full control. We decide, and the Universe delivers what we ask for. We feel superior to some people, but inferior to others. We know that everyone's all together in the human experience, but we can easily become self-righteous. We know that we create our own reality, but others don't know that, or they wouldn't act the way they do. To help them, we may become coaches, healers, and teachers; yet we still feel separate from God, and project blame and criticism.

What keeps us stuck at this level is our identification with the physical self and our identification of others as their physical selves. A more expanded awareness is needed to get out of this loop. Let's start to see ourselves as an emanation of Spirit, which uses the body to express Itself in the material world. We realize that if we have created all the good in our life, we have also created all the pain and suffering—and we simply don't know how to resolve it. The only way is to turn to a Higher Power for help.

This step prepares us for the next level, where we have to let go of the control we have worked so hard to achieve.

3. Channel/Conduit Level

Now, we surrender our personal will to the divine will and relinquish control over anything outside of us. In this way, we become a channel through which Source's energy can flow, transforming our self-image. We accept responsibility for what is manifesting because we have created it in Level 2—which has a separation mindset. We no longer hold on to any desired material outcome, but instead focus on the qualities those outcomes would make us feel. We can be grateful for the experiences that caused us to surrender, because everything has been contributing to our evolution to a higher consciousness. We have now touched this consciousness where we simply cannot feel any resentment or anger about anything that was done to us—since it has advanced us spiritually. Here's where we are starting to see through the eyes of Spirit. The Divine Mind knows that no harm exists, because our material life is just a script we are playing out for the purpose of attaining a closer relationship with our true Self.

4. **Union/Oneness Level**

This level is often called Union—which is a misnomer in a way—because really, there is no unifying of anything, only a dissolution of the human self, with the realization of Oneness. There is still a material human expression—or the appearance of what we call a human being—but what dies is the sense of a personal, material self. I prefer the term oneness, because it's something that cannot be divided. We have never been—and never will be—separate from the Divine.

When Jesus said, "You must be born again" (John 3:3), I take it to mean that we die to the human concept again and again. "I die daily," the Apostle Paul wrote (1 Corinthians 15:31)—until all that's left is the Divine. I like to paraphrase these ideas as, "You must die daily and be reborn again." The dying and the rebirth allow the Divine Itself to come into individuation—not an undifferentiated divine consciousness, but your unique individualized divine consciousness.

In Oneness, we realize we are Source energy expressed in form, also expressed as every other form we see. We realize our essence is the same, that the form taken doesn't matter. As God, we are present in every blade of grass and in every person. At the deepest level, we are one.

If you took a brick of gold and made it into rings, bracelets, and coins, gold is the very substance they are all made of, and the form they have taken cannot be separated from their substance, which is gold. You can destroy the form, but the gold always remains, to take on another form. The ring is the form; gold is the nature of the form; that is, without the gold, a gold ring would not exist. In the same way, we are the form, and Divinity is our true nature. So we forgive ourselves for our false perception of the truth, and see that no harm has been done to our true nature. Instead, we have gained a true perception.

On one level, we are of the utmost importance as expressions of God; simultaneously, on another level we have no importance at all, because we're fictional characters without any reality of our own. Again, where would the ring or bracelet be without the gold? It simply would not exist. In the same way, we would not exist if there were no God, because the Divine constitutes our being.

As personalities, we swing between the first three levels all the time. Once we reach Level-4 consciousness, even if we do fall back into Victim Level because of some occurrence, we can quickly rise out of it and get back to a positive and empowering state of mind by remembering the truth of who we are, even if material circumstances appear difficult or threatening.

Now that we understand the Levels of Consciousness, we can better fathom the Levels of Forgiveness.

LEVELS OF FORGIVENESS

Let's look at the four main consciousness levels again. We can correlate them with the levels of forgiveness— Reactional, Transactional, Transformational, and Transcendental. They testify to where we find ourselves in the growth process. The person or circumstance we are forgiving only serves as a catalyst, to indicate where we are in consciousness.

1. Victim = Reactional
2. Creator = Transactional

THE FOUR LEVELS OF FORGIVENESS

3. Channel = Transformational
4. Oneness = Transcendental

1. **Reactional**

    We forgive at the initial level, which includes other people. They were wrong, and we're a victim. It includes self-pity, resentment, and anger, where we don't deserve this, and they need to suffer. We are stuck in ego, so forgiveness is conditional. They need to repent, and never do it again. The energy of blame is still there; there is no freedom from negative feelings, and no growth. Anytime we see something similar happening to someone else, we flare up, and very likely lash out.

    We might develop addictive or compulsive behaviors; start mistrusting everyone, and project the shadows we've created onto others. We can no longer see the truth of a situation—only our negative interpretation. There is no growth to a higher level.

    For instance, the business agreement you signed was dishonored, so you're angry and disappointed, and threaten your associates with a lawsuit, and then you actually do it. They will likely get angry, too. It's stressful, time-consuming, and expensive; and then the outcome may not be what you expected. Because you didn't take the time to see their perception, consider their difficulties, see their side of things, and so on; none of your actions helped to resolve the situation.

2. **Transactional**

    Taking the same example, when they didn't keep to the agreement you both signed, it still makes you angry or resentful; but you see that they may have had unforeseen difficulties, so you inquire about the reasons, and decide that a lawsuit may not be the best solution. You see their point of view and find a compromise.

You investigate to see if there is anything you could have done differently, to not precipitate this whole experience. You ask *Did I actually help create this?* You are now taking responsibility for your part and for how you feel, without projecting onto others. You decide that even though you're hurt, you are going to learn from the experience and grow.

You will try to find a solution that will work for everyone involved. You realize you have not fully seen the others in their true light; you have not allowed for the conditioning they might have had—their culture, upbringing, and circumstances. You can figure out how to make it a win-win situation that they can accept, without feeling judged or attacked.

In this scenario, we start seeing our own ignorance and lack of awareness that led to this experience, and our own participation in it. Some—maybe even all—blame has been released. We learn by example, seeing how smooth life is for people who are forgiving, and how difficult things are for unforgiving and angry people. We see the possibility of going one way or the other.

Since we still live in the visible three-dimensional world, forgiving and being at peace does not mean that we don't hold people accountable for their actions. We stop destructive behaviors if we can, calling on the proper authorities to prevent further damage. While doing so, we never close our hearts.

Reaching this level is good. Most people don't go beyond this point.

3. **Transformational**

Here is the level of understanding that allows for more compassion and wisdom. We are transforming ourselves physically and spiritually—the real meaning of growth. Physical growth happens *to* you, but spiritual growth happens *through* you.

THE FOUR LEVELS OF FORGIVENESS

Taking the same example of a business agreement, there is another aspect, where we become self-righteous. We still feel hurt, but we pity them, because they don't know any better. We see ourselves as more evolved, more conscious, so we're rising to a higher level, where we can forgive them. They can still make us mad, sad, or upset, but we have compassion—knowing that if they knew better, they would do better. However, we are still not seeing our own ignorance. We don't yet see that this situation is an out-picturing of our consciousness.

Gradually, as we grow, we can appreciate them for being the catalyst for us becoming a wiser and better person. We realize that painful experiences are there to help us expand our consciousness.

Eventually, we abandon our identification as a personality; we come out of the story where we are just the character in the drama of life, to whom things are being done. We step into the role of the performer playing the part of the character, and also into the role of being the author of the play. When we're identified with the *character*, the experience is painful. When we become the *actor* and *author* of the play, the pain dissolves because we see the outcome—the last act of the play.

As Spirit, we have written the script of the play that we are now acting out, together with all the characters that are in our life. They are also playing their parts to help us get to the last act, where we are victorious. They are the main characters in their own play, while being supporting characters in ours.

We're nearing Transcendence when we realize that we are all just playing our parts in a divine drama that we co-created and signed up for. Everyone has to play their scripted parts, just as we have to play ours.

When we can see the role that others have played in our awakening to higher values, we become grateful, we bless them, and we wish them the very best. We feel that shift. We can see that on a soul level, they are a part of us. No real harm has been done, and any seeming harm on the human level has been for our highest good. The feeling of freedom we get at this point is hard to describe. I remember this feeling when I finally healed all the levels relating to the painful aspects of my husband's passing; I was truly grateful for starting on a spiritual path that was irreversible.

4. Transcendental

This is the final level. Transcendence is reached through embodying Truth principles, which means not only intellectually believing, but *knowing*, beyond the shadow of a doubt, that these principles are true. Some of these core principles are:

- There is only one Life, whole and complete—and it is Love.
- Life unfolds according to spiritual law.
- All we could ever want or need is already within us.
- We are fully supported and cared for—as is all life.

Going through all the previous levels is an absolutely necessary part of growth. Here, the meaning of the word *forgiveness* changes. Transcendence is the realization that there is only One Self, which would never harm Itself, so there is no wrong to forgive.

The One Self is divine in nature and is already whole and complete goodness. The many aspects we apply to It—such as joy, peace, beauty, harmony, appreciation, safety, kindness—all boil down to Love. Love can't be anything but loving; there can be no hate, no attack, no hurt. Those hurts can't exist in the Divine Self—and you are It. Its nature is infinite, eternal Love, and absolute Truth. Therefore, lies—expressed as betrayal or abandonment—can't exist.

The realization of the One Self means that there is no other self to harm or be harmed. The whole concept of harm is an illusion. On this level, there is no need for forgiveness, because there is nothing to forgive since no harm has occurred. Here, we are beyond polarities, beyond duality.

In my own life, after years of trying to forgive and get over the pain of my son's death, I finally understood that last bit— even if only intellectually. Then, through grace, I was granted the remembrance of the time when I was a child and I had actually asked to learn unconditional forgiveness after reading that story. This realization led to a total acceptance of my responsibility for my experience. No vestige of blame, anger, or incomprehension remained. I was free, seeing the perpetrator as the divine being that he truly is.

When we have incrementally gone through each level of forgiveness, until we've reached the place where there is no longer any wrong that happened, we are peaceful, and grateful to the people who played their role in getting us to that place of peace. That's a place of undeniable and permanent healing and liberation—because this liberation is not freedom *from* anything, it's the ability to stand tall in the presence of everything. You see it all and it doesn't touch you.

PART 2

THE ASCENSION PATH
OF FORGIVENESS

CHAPTER 7

LEVEL 1—FORGIVENESS AS VICTIM

A young murderer's story:

A young kid, 14 years old, wanted to get into a gang. The initiation rite for entering the gang was to shoot somebody. He shot a kid he didn't know. He was apprehended, brought to trial, and convicted. Just before he was taken away in handcuffs, the mother of the boy who was shot stands up, looks him in the eye, and says, "I'm going to kill you," and then sits down.

After being in prison for a year or so, the boy is visited by that mother, and he's frightened. She says, "I've just got to talk with you." They have a little bit of conversation, and before leaving she asks, "Do you need anything? Cigarettes?" And she gives him a little money. She starts to visit him every few months, and over the course of three or four years, she visits him more regularly, talking with him.

When he's about to get out at the age of 17 or 18, she asks, "What are you going to do?" and he says, "I have no idea. I have no family, no nothing." And she says, "Well, I've got a friend who has a little factory—maybe I can help you get a job."

She makes arrangements with the parole officer. Then she asks, "Where are you going to stay?" and he says, "I don't know where I'm going to go." And she says, *"I have a spare room where you can stay."*

So he goes to live in her house, and takes this job. After about six months, she says, "I really need to talk with you. Come into the living room. Sit down, let's talk." She looks at him and says, "Remember that day in court when you were convicted of murdering my son for no reason at all, to get into your gang, and I stood up and said, "I'm going to kill you"?

"Yes ma'am, I'll never forget that day," he says.

She looks back and says, "Well, I have. You see, I didn't want a boy who could kill in cold blood like that to continue to exist in this world. So I set about visiting you, bringing you things, and taking care of you. And now I got you a job and a place to live, because I don't have anybody anymore. My son is gone and he was the only person in my life. I set about changing you, and you're not that same person anymore. But I don't have anybody, and I want to know if you'd stay here. I'm in need of a son, and I want to know if I can adopt you."

And he said yes, and she did.

CONSCIOUSNESS AT VICTIM LEVEL

As discussed in the last chapter, we are always at a certain level of consciousness, and when we address only a particular aspect of our life—such as forgiveness, love, health, work, etc.—it will always mirror the state of consciousness we are in. At the level of Victim, we usually see life as happening *to* us. We see ourselves as being victimized by external powers and forces—our family, our past, our partner, government, economy, history, society, God—whatever it is, we perceive it as an outside power. At this

LEVEL 1—FORGIVENESS AS VICTIM

stage, it's important to be understanding and compassionate with ourselves.

So even though there are bigger concepts we'll get to eventually, and even though there is a grander perspective from which to look at life, it's important that we don't skip over how we really feel. It's important to feel what we really feel as a reaction.

You have full permission to be at this level. Feel everything, and grasp the value of this early stage of your development. If you want revenge, if you are angry, if you are sad, if you just want to die, I'm giving you permission to feel all of that, and you need to give yourself the same. Be consciously present with all that it means to be at the Victim level. You've got to fully clean out a wound before you can put a bandage over it.

This first stage is a belief of being separate from Source energy; it feels powerless. We take little to no responsibility for anything. We pray to God in Heaven to give us things, to fix things, to do things for us. Everyone else has power, and we don't have any, so we also ask others to fix things, to heal us. Conceptually, we believe God is good, but when we experience adversity, then even God has abandoned us. It's legitimate to feel that.

Finally, at some point, the pain and discomfort are so great that we start seeing the limits of being a victim, so we strive to make some changes. That has to start with a realization that these feelings are generated by us—not by anyone else or by any external situation. Nobody, and nothing outside of us, has the power to make us feel anything. It's our perception, our interpretation—our story about the condition—that generates those feelings. Unless we change them, they become our shadows and stop our progress. Forgive and embrace that part of you that's in resistance. Take conscious stock of all the feelings stirred up in you. That's a critical piece before taking the next step.

There is a difference between having an experience of being victimized, and identifying yourself as a victim. Anyone can have the experience of being a victim at any level of consciousness; but your self-identification is what matters. There are two aspects to being a victim: 1) you see yourself as the victim who has no power, you blame others, and you take no responsibility in the matter, and 2) you are the victim who is searching for ways to get out of it.

At Victim level, you're not in charge of your life. Many people in Victim consciousness who have had a religious upbringing will claim they are surrendering to God, but they haven't yet claimed their authority; they haven't taken responsibility. They haven't seen themselves as sovereign in their lives, because they think it's blasphemy to see oneself as one with God. If they try to surrender at Victim Level, nothing changes; they're still a victim. The only way out of victimhood is claiming control and taking responsibility.

It's not beneficial to skip levels, so now you must go through the stage of Creator first. One of the short-cuts people do—especially spiritually minded people—is to try to jump ahead, right into accessing higher, spiritual ideas and consciousness, when they have not addressed the lower level of really feeling the pain of the victim. Then and only then can they learn to be Creators.

Be patient. Keep in mind that the stages of consciousness are not a progression from the lower to the higher; we go back and forth from one level to another—many times a day sometimes, depending on circumstances and on which area of life is being triggered. This equally applies to forgiveness. Unless we have engaged all the dimensions of our being into the process of forgiveness—and that means the mental, emotional, and physical aspects—forgiveness may not be complete, and similar situations will arise.

Remember, forgiveness is a choice: You either choose to stay stuck in bitterness, anger, and resentment, or you choose to move forward by letting go. The perpetrators don't deserve it—but then, none of us deserves to be forgiven. And yet, isn't that what we ask of God all the time? God forgives unconditionally and infinitely, never asking if we're going to do it again, never saying we don't deserve it. Can we not do the same for our fellow man?

In my own life, initially I failed in my attempts to forgive, but each time taught me something. When it came to what had happened to my husband, I didn't want to feel all of that again. I believed it was wrong to feel all that hate, anger, and condemnation; it was a sin—not Christian. Therefore, I avoided the whole issue, and tried to forgive by retreating into spirituality. I felt guilty about my feelings of vindictiveness and animosity whenever I recalled their heartlessness and barbarism. But the hurt and grief grew worse, not better. I couldn't talk to anyone about it—not even my son—and that might have had an influence on how he was able to process his father's death. I did the best I could with what I had at the time; but I would have spared myself years of suffering had I had all the tools I now have. That's why I am passing this information on to you.

ASPECTS OF FORGIVENESS FROM VICTIM LEVEL

Let's look more closely at the example of a partner or spouse who has betrayed you. It could be any person you most need to forgive for emotional, mental, or physical wounds. I invite you to work through the rest of this chapter and the following ones, with that person as the object. Be attentive to your own reactions or failures to respond. You can start healing the whole issue as you read this.

When there is betrayal, you feel totally crushed. This happened through no fault of your own. *How could my partner do this to me?* Maybe you hesitate to confront the person, because you're afraid of the reaction you'll get, and you wonder if the person will leave. But the thought of the lies continuing is unbearable. You find yourself watching every move; each time there's a business dinner you wonder if it's not a rendezvous with that homewrecker.

When you start getting angry, realizing you don't deserve this, then you see your partner as untrustworthy, egocentric, and uncaring. You see that this person you love has abandoned you, and has no respect for you. It's healthy to be in this mindset—to feel all the feelings. Once your emotions have been processed, they can move through and out of you.

Now, maybe you decide to confront your partner. You feel badly treated, but you don't want your life disrupted. You're more invested in convenience and security than in expressing your fundamental needs. You don't want to be left alone. So you do your best to forgive, and take at face value the lame excuses and promises you hear, that it's over. But you also realize that you have to do some introspection regarding the real reasons why it happened. At this point, you'll discover that you had some responsibility for it.

Make sure you go through the venting of all your real and true feelings first. If you're repressing them, when you do the introspection to see the real reasons, instead of it being a healing process, it just becomes another way in which you are being wounded again and blaming yourself. If that's the case, it becomes an act of self-violence—making yourself wrong—which is not at all the same thing as taking responsibility.

As you start looking more deeply at what could have led to that betrayal, almost always you'll find some things that you could have done differently. Maybe there were signs earlier that you didn't want to recognize; you were afraid of jeopardizing the relationship. You could have been ignorant; lied to yourself; felt powerless, weak, or insecure. Those parts of you sabotaged your inner knowing—that you should have confronted your partner much earlier, as soon as you felt something was wrong. You did not value yourself enough to stand up for yourself. This is the beginning of rising out of being

LEVEL 1—FORGIVENESS AS VICTIM

a powerless victim and seeing the need to forgive the parts of you that were foolish, insecure, unaware, or weak. Have compassion for yourself.

Victimhood is a very perilous stage where you don't want to stay, because it can become self-destructive, or it can become outer-destructive. So either you'll be criticizing yourself, not standing up for yourself, saying *I'm unworthy*, and *I'm not good enough*; or, it can become disapproval of others, with anger and attacks.

If somebody steps on your toe, you don't think *Well, the pain is actually a signal coming from my brain, so it's not really caused by the person*. No! You tell that individual *Stop that! Get off my toe! You're hurting me!*

Even taking revenge is a higher frequency than depression. But don't act it out—don't take revenge on people. Lock yourself up in your room and scream, call them names, pound your pillows. When your rage is totally spent, recognize the power you had to express all your feelings and still retain control over yourself. There was a little piece of your awareness witnessing that rage. You have felt all the feelings, and you are the master of them. From this new place of calm, reflect on some constructive action you can take. You don't need to step on the person's toe in return, but you do need to say *Get off my toe!* That is a very empowering action to help the victim that you feel you are, without overtly and explicitly attacking the person. You could have a conversation about it, and set boundaries. You don't want that individual to continue making your life miserable.

So as you sincerely forgive yourself, release the betrayer, too. Clearly state the new expectations you have for your relationship to continue in a solid and sustainable way. Now it's all out in the open. Listen to what the other person is saying, have compassion and acceptance—and also take really good care of yourself. Finally, you are ready and willing to let go. You forgive because you're not going to keep yourself in a state of suffering.

Acknowledge both your feelings and the other person's feelings, which can include allowing one of you to move out. Creating the life you want is within your power. Perhaps you can begin to understand the reasons that kept you stuck as a victim for so long. What were the pay-offs? You did not have to think too much about finances if you both had a job and paid the mortgage and bills. Maybe your partner took care of those details. The headaches of your car breaking down were not yours because there was another car to borrow if needed. You had a companion to talk to when you came home in the evenings, and you had someone to plan your holidays with. Life alone would be very different. But all along, a part of you was sacrificed for comfort and convenience, when you were actually unhappy. You are beginning to see that you no longer want to ignore that part of yourself.

A relationship can only work well when each person feels whole and fulfilled as an individual, and each recognizes the need for the other to be whole and fulfilled as an individual also. If you are not ready to take full responsibility and forgive yourself for your lack of discernment and for whatever else you have discovered, as well as to forgive the other person's transgression, then creating the new life you really want will simply not be possible. State your own desires, needs, and values, which must be respected in the future. Equally hear and respect the other person's needs. When you do this, you will both be on the right path.

Exercise: Being Forgiveness

When we want to forgive, figuring out how to get there is always the place where we get stuck. An easier approach is to use your intention and attention to develop a state of being that is an aspect of the Divine.

LEVEL 1—FORGIVENESS AS VICTIM

First, decide to be *coming from*—rather than *getting to*—a specific state of being, in this case, of being *Forgiveness*. So, declare *I AM FORGIVENESS* for a minute or two, internally or out loud, and allow yourself to fully feel and embrace that state of being.

Do this right before falling asleep, so it's the last thought on your mind, which won't be interfered with by life's happenings for the next few hours. And do it again, for a couple of minutes when waking up. Also, anytime the person or event comes to mind, put your full attention on yourself exclusively.

This will fill your being with forgiveness, leaving no room for remembering the wrong. When practicing this consistently, you'll find that you're becoming a different state of being. Then, when the person or situation comes to mind, there is no longer the same charge around it, and it may come up much less frequently.

Repeat this practice until the charge completely disappears, and you are able to perceive the blessing that the event has been for your own evolution.

How to Forgive Yourself

At first, forgiving yourself is not even an option on the table. You see yourself as a total victim, with nothing that needs forgiving. That's a pattern, so when you recognize it for what it is, you can release it.

Examining every aspect of the situation and what could have been your part in it is definitely an important step to take. Were there any signs that you ignored? Did you say or do something that was better left unsaid? Did you keep silent when you should have spoken up? Where did you not trust your guidance, or not ask for what you needed? Did you repress your real feelings and desires? Were you afraid of being judged too needy, or incompetent? That's a pattern that often starts in childhood—a teacher criticizes our work; our parents say we're being selfish when we demand what we want; or we get beaten up by a bully in school. We feel rejected, victimized, a failure, or unworthy. Because we don't like these feelings, we may decide to become a helper to others, to be generous, or to work hard in school and so to be loved, accepted, and rewarded. And that strategy is wonderful, because we do get the recognition we crave, and we develop some really good qualities that help us move forward in life. We thrive. We become a person who's independent, capable, kind, and giving.

But all that is at the expense of rejecting other qualities that we also need—but have judged as bad until now—because they caused us pain in the past. At some point, our life gets out of balance—things that used to work don't work any longer—and we realize we must make some changes. We feel victimized, yet we also feel bad about the way we are showing up. We don't like feeling worthless, stupid, helpless, gullible, or a failure. There is real pain there that we don't want to disregard, and all those parts of us that have been rejected are now sabotaging us. In order to make progress, we need to recognize their inherent value, and integrate them as beneficial and helpful aspects of us.

Here is where it's time to make the decision to start acting differently from how you did before. Become clear about what you want your life to look like. Have that difficult conversation you have been avoiding. Set some boundaries that may not have been clear before. Do whatever will make your situation the one you really, really want.

You'll also quickly realize that if people have hurt you once, you will keep hurting *yourself* over and over by not forgiving them. Stop wasting energy blaming others. Search for places where you are condemning yourself in any way, thinking it was your fault. Stop

LEVEL 1—FORGIVENESS AS VICTIM

that violence against yourself, and appreciate those shadow parts of you. They will allow you to access the peace, joy, wisdom, and power you always wanted.

If your partner apologizes and expresses regrets, a whole different dynamic may open up. You also have to feel the grief, the guilt, and the pain you caused; and then finally feel remorse. It's only through feeling everything that it all can be transformed. Ultimately, be sure to forgive yourself in the process.

It is said that when you die and have your life review, one of the things you do is to go back and re-experience the pain you have caused other people, which you did not fully feel at the time. It's very important to become aware of every emotion and feeling, so that nothing gets repressed. Bring it all into full consciousness.

Forgiving groups, institutions, and organizations

Ask yourself: *Has this betrayal created any global wounds*? In other words, if the person who has hurt you is a man, do you now feel distrust about men in general? If it's a woman, do you distrust all women? That perception is a lie that must be healed, by forgiving the whole gender.

When people come out of victimhood in their private lives, and embrace their truth—standing up for what they want and refusing to be victimized by their partner—then they also see that they're not victims of situations and institutions that have been operating for centuries. It seems that nothing can be done to obtain integrity and justice; but we *can* reclaim our power and demand changes. We are at a turning point in human history where abuse, conflict, and murder will no longer be acceptable, because people will no longer allow it.

We have had an example of this in Spain. In the summer of 2018, a woman was gang-raped by five men, and they were given light sentences because the judges (all men) called it "sexual abuse" rather than rape. But a huge manifestation resulted, which went on for days. All the women were out on the streets protesting until a new harsher judgment for rape was declared! But the shift didn't stop there. They went on clamoring for the judges who made the ruling to be thrown out. It was an enormous protest; they actually managed to have the laws around that issue changed.

Blaming God

When something bad happens, do you blame God for your situation? Maybe you think you are being punished by God for some misdemeanor, and that's why your partner cheated on you. Or, you wonder why God didn't stop this terrible thing from happening, when He's so much more powerful than you are.

In that case, *God* represents a power that's acting upon us from the outside, like a parent. At this stage, our concept of a God outside of us is almost always a projection of our own unhealed parental issues. The truth is, there is no such thing as a God who's going to punish you for having your feelings. It's okay to feel all of that. If your upbringing was religious, however, you may be terrified to feel that way: Now you're not only a sinner, but also angry at God, so it makes you twice as bad. This can become very convoluted and difficult, so just know that it's all only your limited perception of what God really is, plus an unhealed pattern of your parental issues. Simply be present to what's arising—the fear, the anxiety, and so forth—and then *forgive God*, just as you would forgive a parent.

Forgiving a person who's deceased

If someone no longer living has hurt you, remember that forgiveness is primarily for *you*, not for the other person. When the person is no longer here, there can be a lot of repressed feelings. You may have feelings of powerlessness, or futility, because this person cannot hear you. You want to be free and unfettered. There's always a way to put these matters right. You can say *I feel so hurt*! Or *I'm such a failure*! Say whatever you need to express. Then, as each issue comes up, love each part of yourself individually. Love is all that is needed. All the work we do with other people can, and must, also be done within ourselves. Try the following exercise to release the tension.

> ## Visualization Exercise
>
> Sit in quiet meditation, and visualize the person alive. Visualize the time when that unforgivable thing happened to you. Now see that this person dwells in the realm of Spirit, where there is no perception of wrong. Imagine just what this individual would say to you now, from that space of new awareness. Just think of a few words, something that will improve your memory of the whole experience. Visualize this person as an expression of Spirit saying these healing words. Even if you can't forget the past, these few words will inspire you to forgive.
>
> Once you have heard this person's spiritual Self say the words to you that you've been longing to hear, remember them. Keep saying them to your own heart to soothe your wounds—for just a minute or two at a time, many times a day. Do this every time you think of this person. Even if it feels inauthentic at first, do it anyway. Even though you still remember that person's bad personality, through constant repetition, the words will become familiar. You'll be visualizing the spiritual identity, not the flawed human person. Over time, the ache in your heart will dissolve. You have given to yourself what no one else can ever give you: love. Love comes from within you and to you, and now Love can expand from you to all.

WHY WE STAY AT VICTIM LEVEL

When we're still in the Victim perspective, there are many things to forgive, because things are done to us that we don't like, and we feel powerless to do anything about them. We give away our innate power to parents, or others who seem to have power—to doctors, schools, organizations, even God—asking others to look after us and defend us.

As a victim, we see ourselves as wronged, and it's the perpetrator who is bad; we are the better person. This kind of a superiority complex is often simultaneously mixed with an inferiority complex—we're still the poor miserable victim. We don't truly know where we stand, until we make a decision. We either make ourselves feel better than the other person, who is to blame; or we make ourselves feel less than the other, blaming ourselves.

We stay stuck at this level because we don't really allow ourselves to feel. We create coping mechanisms which cause us either to act out aggressively, or to withdraw and shrink, feeling shame and unworthiness. We repeat that pattern in relationship after relationship. To get unstuck, we must feel all the painful feelings, and then meet our true needs. We can't stay in victimhood forever. It will become so painful that eventually we will want to take charge of our destiny. At a certain point all external support will fail us, and we will be forced by circumstances into taking responsibility.

Until we become conscious of the negative feelings and neutralize them, anything we don't like will throw us back into feeling like a victim again. We finally heal those feelings through focusing on, and giving love, acceptance, and validation—*to ourself*, to the exclusion of anyone else involved in the situation.

It's the consciousness we have that keeps us stuck at Victim level, whatever our age. As mental capacities expand, our understanding

LEVEL 1—FORGIVENESS AS VICTIM

of life and behavior changes, and we see the results of our actions. We realize there are different ways of responding to situations.

For example, let's say you've had a heated argument with someone, and feel so resentful, you can't let go of your viewpoint and forgive, because that would mean you were not "right." For you, being right is more important than letting go of the grudge. Ask yourself: *Why is it so important for me to be right*? The answer may be that if you are right, then you are accepted and valued, and your opinion has worth. In this case, forgiveness may be equated in your mind with a lack of self-worth.

In the absolute realm of the Divine, self-worth and forgiveness are not mutually exclusive. Making an affirmation where they are weaved together would be one way to resolve such a dilemma. And it could be as simple as affirming for yourself, *The more I fully feel what I feel, the quicker I let go of resentment and forgive. And the quicker I forgive and let go of resentment, the more worthy and valuable I feel.*

Moving to the next level takes your willingness to be fully present with what happened. So feel whatever you must towards the other person, however painful this may be—without shame, blame, or apology. Also recognize your responsibility for what happened, without accusing yourself. Now you can see that there are more things in your control than you initially thought. Once you realize that, you'll graduate out of Level 1.

Whatever your issue is, there is a natural evolutionary process that begins to elevate you out of this stage. When you feel fully, not seeking to get rid of a feeling or to judge or resist it, there is a transmutational evolutionary movement that happens, where the feeling evolves to the next feeling up the ladder of emotional resonance. If you feel your anger fully, it doesn't mean you act it out. Then it will begin to rise up to the next level, and reveal to you that underneath the anger there may be disappointment, or deep grief. Then as you feel that fully, too, it will release, revealing another layer and another—until underneath all of that there might be a feeling of empowerment, inspiration, or neutrality. Then that will move you into a more expanded, freer place to start feeling better about yourself.

THE PROCESS FOR MOVING TO THE NEXT LEVEL

Because we are all born as a helpless infant, the Victim level is where we all start our lives. It must be fully owned before we can let go of it. Really owning this level is crucial.

It's like the example of a child who needs to own his birthday gift, a truck with flashing lights and a siren, before letting a younger sibling play with it; but his parents ask him not to be selfish, to share it with his brother—before he has truly owned and taken possession of it. The boy needed time spent with the toy, exploring it and playing with it, before he was ready to let someone else have a turn—and that is normal and as it should be. But when that process is curtailed in this child's development, he may either grow up with very weak boundaries and have a hard time asking for what he wants; or, he could go in the other direction—becoming stingy, because he's still trying to complete the stage of owning, which got interrupted.

In the same way, we need time spent with our Victim self, exploring all the facets of it with curiosity, asking *Why do I feel like this when this person says that? Isn't it interesting that this comes up? And if it comes up, it's a part of me, just like every other part, and it must be useful, because all parts of me are there for a reason!* Journal about it, rather than hiding or pushing it away. It really is a part of us and therefore also a part of the Divine. If we don't like it, it's only because we don't have a true perception of it. Let's try to see those aspects from different angles and fresh viewpoints, which will reveal to us their positive side.

LEVEL 1—FORGIVENESS AS VICTIM

Whatever feelings you have, you won't stay in them forever. Everything in this world changes; so as you forgive from the level where you are, a higher level will be activated. If you don't like where you stand, it's up to you to move to a higher level and understand that if you want your life to look different, you must think and act differently. Take full responsibility for your own responses to events. Examine your ways of being to see if they still serve you. If not, change them.

Everyone has been conditioned by family upbringing; we took on certain qualities and patterns subconsciously, without questioning them. Observing how others successfully manage their lives—with their words, emotions, and actions—teaches us what can be achieved. Adopting those attitudes for ourselves—even when we're not feeling like that, or afraid of doing it—and watching how our life can change for the better, will encourage us to continue experimenting.

As you begin to take action—whether it's to value, respect, and redeem yourself to reclaim your power, or it's an effort to release and forgive someone—it's very likely that more emotions will come up. You might think you've made progress, because you feel more expanded after doing all this work, and you're taking greater care of yourself, and treating yourself better. But suddenly you feel angry or sad again. If this occurs, don't bypass the question *Why am I still angry? I shouldn't still be angry*! Don't push it away, because that would be abusing yourself. You want to stop, feel all your feelings once more, let them move all the way through, and then go back to whatever constructive action of self-empowerment you were doing before.

A parallel between temporal life and spiritual life can be drawn here. A child can't become a successful adult without going through stages of differentiation—like when a child first realizes it's separate from its mother, or when an adolescent sees herself as different from her parents. The teenager has a unique identity, will, desires, and vision for life. That's a step up from before, when everything was done by the parents. In the same way, spiritually we step away from being a victim to see ourselves as sovereign—as a Creator, which is the next level.

It's constructive to journal, writing down all your feelings. Maybe, depending on the circumstances, you can have that difficult conversation, telling the person exactly how you feel and what your expectations are. Then, you can start developing a practice that will ultimately become a habit, of treating yourself—and others!—better than you were treated in the past.

If you were neglected, treat yourself and others with care. If someone stole from you, start practicing generosity. If you were abandoned, spend more time being a faithful companion to yourself, validating and fulfilling your own desires. And then, what you feel when you appreciate and take care of yourself, you can extend to others. Over a period of time, the hurt dissolves. Then, there is no more need for the memory of that person who wronged you even to ever arise. Just by loving the one who was hurt, the person who hurt us is automatically forgiven. Thus, we forgive others by simply loving ourselves.

Letter-Writing Exercise

One way of accomplishing forgiveness is to write a letter to your partner or spouse who has betrayed you (which you will never send!) in which you detail every single thing you have experienced, and how you feel about it. Be really honest and *non*spiritual about doing this. Then fold it up and hide it—which is a symbolic gesture of what we do with our emotions.

Take it out the next day and read it over. Feel all the feelings it brings up, and then add more to the letter, making it even stronger. Then put it away once more.

The next day, reread it again, and feel all of it fully. Then make a decision: that you want to be done with these emotions—for good! Finally, either make a fire in your backyard and ceremoniously burn the letter there, or hold it over a large metal saucepan, and put a match to it. Feel the intensity of letting all the words, feelings, and emotions go as you feel the heat of the flames. It's a challenge to release it all, because you've built an identity from all of these old feelings of anger, hate, unworthiness, and so on. Watching them being consumed and turning to ash really helps.

Depending on the issue you're dealing with, you could also write a letter to any and all parties that may be involved in the problem. So you could be forgiving your spouse, but if it brought up some additional stuff about your parents, write to them, too. Or write to God, if you feel betrayed by God. Don't hold back. Fully express yourself.

Perhaps you could also write to yourself, or some part of yourself—such as your inner child—where you validate that kid for every feeling, apologize for what happened, and assure that child that now you're always going to provide protection. Give that part of yourself whatever is needed so that your inner child feels fully heard, understood, safe, loved, and validated.

CHAPTER 8

LEVEL 2—FORGIVENESS AS CREATOR

Always forgive your enemies—nothing annoys them so much!
—Oscar Wilde

CONSCIOUSNESS AT CREATOR LEVEL

In the last chapter, where we discussed forgiveness at the level of victimhood, you gave yourself permission to fully acknowledge what happened; to embrace all that you were feeling; to take some positive affirming actions for yourself; and to work towards releasing the other person. Whatever your feelings were, they were exactly what was needed to make you decide that you could, and would, take control of your life. Having control also means taking responsibility.

Now you can begin to open to a grander perspective. You know you are no longer a victim, so you're ready to move forward. Now you're reclaiming your power as Creator, as someone who's in control. Don't skip ahead, but stay in this level and own it. What you are learning now is that you can act upon your life, instead of being a victim of life. Here, you have full permission to own the power of being in control, of being the Creator of your reality.

We're not going to do a spiritual bypass—saying that it's wrong to manipulate and control in order to manifest whatever you want. The whole point of this stage is to feel empowered and in control. We're just going to fully forgive at this level. That doesn't mean that you are letting people off the hook, but simply that you're taking back your power as Creator of your life.

Intrinsic in that power is taking responsibility for how you have helped to create the situation of betrayal—or whatever it is that you're working through. As we take more control, we can start forgiving others, because we are gaining a higher understanding of what life is about—of who we are and who they are. Your forgiveness as a victim was mainly mental, very much dependent on their apology or redress, or because you were taught you should forgive. Now that you have let go of victimhood to some extent, it will lead you to doing more, creating or manifesting conditions you prefer, and believing that you have the power to change what you don't like.

We start by employing metaphysical laws—that is, mental and emotional laws—to manipulate material forms. The Creator stage is where the Law of Attraction really comes into play; it lives at this level, where we are using our mental, emotional, and physical aspects—thinking, feeling, and doing—to manifest a reality other than the one imposed upon us. We become good at manipulating people and conditions, using the power we have to obtain justice, or to attain proper amends. All of this is great, and grounds us in the Creator Level of being, where we can begin to have compassion for the offender. We now feel superior, because we know we can control our experience. But all of this has nothing to do, as yet, with spiritual laws, which only come into play later, when transitioning into the Channel Level.

LEVEL 2—FORGIVENESS AS CREATOR

There are three intermediate stages here:
1. The Creator as a child—just wanting what you want and demanding it;
2. The Creator as the adolescent—really starting to see yourself as different from your parents and knowing that you have a legitimate say in what you want;
3. The mature Creator with greater awareness—seeing that there is something else at play beyond your own personality.

This stage is a powerful and important one, not to be neglected. Until you experience having control and power, you can't truly move to the stage of surrendering that control. You have to have a pencil in your hand in order to let go of it. Taking control over yourself and your life is always good; it moves you deeper into Level 2.

So it's okay to claim control. Don't rush into letting go of it. Even though you've been told it's not spiritual—it's not heart-centered, it's selfish, or it's calculating. Maybe you had a very controlling parent or authority figure in your life, and so you've lived your life trying *not* to be controlling. That's a shadow; and that's part of the problem.

You need to take control of your life and feel what that feels like. Get the growth it gives you—the healing of your ego, and ultimately, of your heart. Then you can begin to let go. You'll know how to take control when you need it, and how to let go when something is not serving you.

As co-creators, we realize we have power. We can change conditions by controlling people and situations. We manifest our reality. Nevertheless, since suffering is also our reality, we must have created that, too. But we don't know how to resolve it. If we ever believed in God, here's where we may be rejecting that whole idea, since *we* have the power, and *we* are the one creating results. Or, if we still believe in God, then God is a power we can manipulate on the metaphysical level of mind over matter; we no longer need God because we believe we are the one in control. God is there to serve our desires.

As we get results through control, we can become attached to outcomes—to our idea of what should or shouldn't be. This attachment limits our ability to express our true, full potential of what's trying to emerge through us. It can lead to things not working out well, causing frustration, anxiety and depression.

As entrepreneurs, teachers, speakers, and healers we help and fix others. We have control over our life, and over others' lives. We live from a place of having control, and that's as it should be in this stage. Without this stage first, we could never successfully get to the next level, the Channel Level. When we discover a Power higher than ourselves, only then can we relax, and surrender to it.

ASPECTS OF FORGIVENESS FROM THE CREATOR LEVEL

Forgiving others

Let's take the same example of betrayal as before (you can work with the people or situation you chose in Chapter 7). You are now aware of your own responsibility in that event, and even if you forgave because you know more, or they don't know any better, you are still judging them. You are not yet seeing your own ignorance of a higher reality—that they are just a reflection of your consciousness. At this level, you are more aware of your power, so you will not let them ruin your life. You do your best to forgive, and as that raises your consciousness, you realize with gratitude that you have expanded and grown in understanding. You find relief, and even wish them the very best. You're willing to bless them, to wish them luck with their growth—so long as they keep away from you! You decide you are going to think positive thoughts about them, so that you can remain peaceful.

At this level, you are seeking to feel more powerful over conditions or situations. Here, it becomes a power struggle to gain greater power and control over people and conditions, rather than just feeling superior. Reclaiming your power and control, using it and owning it is crucial. Not getting caught in a power struggle is just as important.

At this point, we still hold on to blame, we still see the situation, but we think we can exert some control over it—changing others, or the circumstances. We see the problem as largely outside of us, so we manipulate people and conditions. We are still not fully taking responsibility for our experience, nor realizing it's almost entirely an inside job.

In this level, we haven't yet realized that all forgiveness is self-forgiveness—because all areas where we are triggered are shadows—parts of ourselves that need to be seen, heard, understood, loved, and embraced, so that they can be redeemed as a part of Divinity. As Jesus said to his disciples, "Love your enemies" (see Matthew 5:44–45); he also asserted, "the enemy is in your own household" (see Matthew 10:36)—which I interpret to mean that the enemy is within our own consciousness. It's all those shadow parts of us that we dislike and want to get rid of. (Now is a good time to go through the Shadow Exercise in Chapter 3 again.)

To the extent that you can take control over conditions in a constructive way, at this stage you want to do that. That's owning your power. You absolutely want to take control over conditions that caused the problem, to whatever extent you can. This is where you really need the Serenity Prayer: *God, grant me the serenity to accept the things I cannot change, the courage to change the things I can, and the wisdom to know the difference.*

From the self-righteous stance of *I'm better than you*, your forgiveness can rise to the transformational level (Level 3)—being able to see an opportunity for spiritual advancement. This is when you see the need for *you* to change in some way to free you from the pain, because you realize you are its creator. What you have created, you can un-create, by becoming someone different. You forgive, because you can see this as an opportunity to learn, to not make the same mistakes again; you see you have become more aware and you have grown. It's not a *blame the victim* mentality, but a greater level of conscious responsibility, so you don't revert to the same old patterns of behavior. By becoming aware, you can now change your beliefs and expectations, and rewrite the map you were living before to create a new, more empowering one.

In the story of Mary, who forgave her daughter Claire for her behavior towards her deceased husband (in Chapter 3), Mary suffered financial loss because she stayed at Victim Level. She did not rise into Creator consciousness because she didn't recognize that she had partial responsibility. She skipped Level 2, Creator, and went straight into Level 3, where God, Love, is all there is—but because she wasn't ready, she needed to go back to the work of Level 2. Even if it's true that *God is all there is, so we are whole, perfect and complete,* that will never work from the level of Victim or Creator. The reason for this is we've missed out on feeling remorse for our actions, and the pain the other person must feel, as well as our own pain, shame, anger, and so forth. It is necessary to forgive at each of these stages in order to reach a level of deep understanding. If we don't thoroughly go through this process, those unresolved emotions will block us farther up the road.

Victims have more of a wishbone than a backbone, which a Creator learns to develop. Mary was still afraid of what Claire would think about her if she legally protected her interests. At Level 2, you need to create healthy boundaries where you are not letting yourself be victimized, where you are able to say no. You forgive people but you don't let them off the hook; you need to make sure you're

LEVEL 2—FORGIVENESS AS CREATOR

protected. Being in control is about taking full responsibility for your life. That way, when you move to Level 3 and you are forgiving at deeper levels, you bring with you the ability to set healthy boundaries and to get what you need.

This is really important: heart-centered people often let themselves be taken advantage of, because it feels bad to be demanding agreements and holding people accountable. We often don't stand up for what is right and for what we need, in the name of some high concept of love. But the result is always suffering because we're getting short-changed. The relationship is not helped at all; in fact, it gets worse because we have skipped Level 2 and feel like a victim again.

Here is where we begin to discern what is safe and what isn't, and ultimately find power and security within ourselves—which is absolutely necessary before we can let go of the defense mechanisms we created in the Victim stage. It's really your sacred responsibility to manifest a life where you feel empowered.

When we skip over a level, forgiveness fails. For example, I tried to forgive someone for years. I suffered financial loss because I had not owned the Creator Level yet. I felt at fault, because I was already on a spiritual path after my husband's passing. I had shadows of being mean, uncharitable, and feeling bad for believing the worst about others. I didn't take the proper actions to protect myself, so I was knocked back to Level 1, feeling like a victim again.

It's critical that we take care of ourselves at each level. In order to see my blind spots, I did the work on my shadows. I began to see all the positive—even if difficult—aspects of the situation. Potentially, I saw that they could move me up the spiritual spiral; so when the next situation arose, I was able to take full responsibility for what I wanted and needed, placing it on a legal and binding basis.

To become more aware of where you stand, make a list of the people you need to forgive and what they did. Ask *What is my present level of forgiveness for each of them? Is there still some resentment?* If you think there is no one and nothing to forgive, ask yourself *What people do I have negative feelings about when I think of them, and why*? Those feelings also need forgiveness! New names might come up, of people you haven't thought about in years. Pay attention!

Choosing to forgive while refusing to stay the victim is very powerful. It's an individual act from the second level of consciousness, not requiring any participation from the abuser. It takes two to have a reconciliation, but only one to choose to forgive. The other person doesn't even have to know about it.

Forgiving yourself

Now that you have become more aware of your role in the situation, and also, you've forgiven yourself at a lower level for being naïve or stupid, you realize that as Creator, you can take responsibility for what you did and why you did it, and forgive yourself at this new level. With your present awareness, forgive through unconditional acceptance of every part of you, whatever it looks like, as a part of Divinity that forgot Its true nature. Ultimately, everything is serving our evolution.

Like a baby who abandons crawling once walking is mastered, you abandon old beliefs and expectations you held as a Victim, adopting new beliefs that will get you to a place of peace and contentment. In the Creator stage, you have a sense of management—a sense of the ability to get things done, to manifest things. The hallmark of this stage is owning your power to design your life. You no longer believe life is happening *to* you; *you* are now happening to life. You take responsibility for the good as well as the bad. You must detect how you're responsible for creating everything in your life. You don't play the blame game, but maintain your awareness of the patterns underlying your actions. That's the whole point of the introspection. You now begin to create a vision of how you are going to make your life better. That's critical: You

LEVEL 2—FORGIVENESS AS CREATOR

can't become a Creator until you take 100 percent responsibility for your experiences, without any projections upon anyone else.

Forgiving a person who's deceased

From Level 2, you no longer let anything others have said or done influence you. Now, you can superimpose what you want on them. What new level of control would you exert over your conditions and actions, to live more fully with regard to these people who are not here anymore to stop you, judge you, or block you?

Since *for*-giveness also means *to give forth*, whatever is missing is what you're not giving. So let's say when this person was alive the biggest pain for you was judgment; you felt shamed, like you weren't enough. As a result, you didn't do certain things, didn't try certain things, didn't become a certain way. Now you get to take back that power and take control over those parts of your life again, and start to live as if this individual had no more control over you—because it's true.

As you start to express the energy which has been repressed, that act alone will expand you. It also frees you from a lot of the pain, bitterness, and blockages. That's a very dynamic and active way of forgiving, because it's not just saying *I forgive you*, but also saying *I love you, and I let you go*. Now, you are showing up differently, and you are taking all control back. The other person has no more power.

Forgiving God

When your partner betrayed or abandoned you, you may have thought that the Universe was operating against you. So at this level, you may have thrown away the whole idea of God; or, because you believe you now have all the power, you decide that God is something you can exploit to get your own way. God does as you ask; here you are at the metaphysical level where you begin to apply the laws of mind and manifestation, and you believe you don't really need God, because you're the one with the power to control.

On the other hand, your concept of God evolves at every level, and has to be forgiven. You get to evolve your God from the old version that the Victim consciousness holds—of a mysterious and wrathful God—to the concept of a God that wants you to have more power and control over your life, a God that wants you to have the life you desire. After all, He created you—and doesn't a parent want the very best for His children? If that was your God now, how would you begin to show up in your life? What control would you take concerning the issue you are wrestling with?

WHY WE STAY AT CREATOR LEVEL

This is very satisfying stage—feeling powerful, seeing the good things in life, getting what you want, and helping others with their problems. God is on your side, helping you achieve. You don't yet realize that God is on no one's side, but equally with everyone. You've taken a very powerful step that begins to release the negative energy of victimhood you were holding before. You release everyone, alive or dead, from having control over you.

However, you are still seeing the other person as having done you wrong. But now that you have control, it equally applies to how you want to feel. You don't let anyone else determine that. When you're letting love and generosity flow, you feel better. You can decide to direct all those good feelings to heal the area of animosity where the offenders reside, and to reclaim your ability to fully express the Divinity and love that you are. Wherever God's life-force can't flow *through* you, to prosper all of life around you, it can't flow *into* you, either. That's stagnation—just like when a pond stagnates if there

LEVEL 2—FORGIVENESS AS CREATOR

is no inflow or outflow, and everything in it dies. This energy of sluggishness shows up in your life as mental or emotional dullness, and very often as financial debt.

If you've fully stepped into your role as Creator, you can reach the point where you say *Nobody has the right to close my heart! Only I decide that! You think you can stop my heart from being loving and generous towards you? Never! I'm going to be a bigger and more loving person, because then I feel better about me, and I know that will create even better experiences in my life. And if that's being selfish, great! Then that's what I am.*

THE PROCESS FOR MOVING TO THE NEXT LEVEL

As Creator, you manifest what you want and more and more of it—until the realization dawns that you must have also manifested all the unwelcome things in your life, over which you had no control. If you had not, you could not now be seeing it or experiencing it. You have embodied the truth that nothing can come into your experience except through your consciousness; and getting more stuff to mask your suffering is not working. The experience of betrayal has come up so that you, the Creator of that misperception, can see its divine aspect again. It's therefore up to you to use the tool of forgiveness at this level to reclaim control, ultimately becoming a generative being again—where nobody and nothing can stop you from expressing who you really are: an expression of Divinity.

You can now say to anyone *You were wrong, but that's your problem! I am powerful and can create the life I want, despite what you did.* That's what forgiveness is, at this level. Now you have to exert that power and control so that it visibly manifests for you.

Level 1 was all about feeling our feelings, expressing them, getting clear on what we want and validating ourselves, which led to taking some responsibility and control. So now we are taking full power and control over conditions and people. We must start taking specific actions that make us feel empowered—and take them consistently, in every instance and every area of our life—so as to create new habits of how we respond when something distressing happens.

We need to design a life for ourselves that asks *If I had full control, how would I act in this circumstance? How would I think, how would I speak? How would I feel? How would I show up differently from before?* Acting as if we were that calm, assured, secure, and confident person is powerful, and yields amazing results. We look at the various spheres of our lives where we operate—wealth, work, relationships, and personal development—and ask *How can I show up better in each of these areas?*

We also need to create healthy boundaries, so that we won't be overstepped by our partner, spouse, kids, friends, or colleagues. Boundaries help us avoid many potential problems. We are very clear about our own values and expectations, and about what we allow, or deem unacceptable. That's speaking our truth! It could also be a specific conversation we have as soon as we feel something is not quite right, rather than keeping silent and hoping it was just a one-time thing.

We need to consciously design the life we want, because it will never just happen on its own; other people's agendas will take precedence unless we have an agenda that we keep, no matter what. That means we ask and stand up for what we need—put it in writing, make contracts, do everything legally, etc.—and we don't let go of that.

CHAPTER 9

LEVEL 3—FORGIVENESS AS CHANNEL

The story of Holocaust survivor, Eva Mozes Kor:

I was born in 1934, one of a pair of twins. We lived in Romania, and our whole family was taken by the Nazis in cattle wagons, to an unknown destination.

On arrival, down on the platform, a Nazi noticed we were twins, pulled my mother away, and the last I remember was her arms stretched out to us in despair. Miriam and I were crying.

We would be Mengele's twins—and only later we found out what that meant.

I was used in two types of experiments. Mondays, Wednesdays, Fridays, they would put us naked in a room with many other twins, up to 8 hours a day. They measured every part of my body, comparing it to my twin sister's, and then to charts. On alternate days, they would take us to a blood lab, take a lot of blood from my left arm and give me a minimum of five injections in the right arm. Even today we don't know what those contained.

One day I became very ill, with high fever, huge red spots covering my body, my legs and arms swollen and very painful. I was taken to hospital, another barrack filled with people who looked more dead than alive. Next morning, Mengele declared: "Too bad! She's so young. She has only two weeks to live."

FORGIVENESS—A PATH TO CREATE MIRACLES

For the following two weeks, I have only one clear memory: crawling on the floor because I no longer could walk, to reach a faucet with water at the other end of the barrack. I would fade in and out of consciousness, telling myself "I must survive! I must survive!" Finally, my fever broke and I was taken back to Miriam, who was sitting on the bed staring into space. I asked her, "What happened?" She said, "I can't talk about it."

She never talked about Auschwitz until 1985, in Israel, when she developed a severe kidney infection. The doctors found that Miriam's kidneys never grew larger than the size of a 10-year-old child. Later, they failed and I donated my left kidney. A year later, she developed cancer in the bladder, but we never found the Auschwitz files and what was injected; and Miriam died.

We were then working on a documentary done by German television about the Mengele twins, where Dr. Munch, a Nazi doctor from Auschwitz, appeared. I got his telephone number, called him, and he invited me to Germany where I asked him many questions. He said this was a nightmare he lived with every day of his life. He was stationed outside the gas chamber looking through a peephole, while people were dying. When nobody moved, he had to sign one death certificate. No names, just the number of people that they murdered.

I wanted him to sign a document of just what he had told me, but I wanted it signed at the ruins of the gas chamber in Auschwitz. I asked him to go there with me to watch the film of the liberation of the camp. He immediately agreed.

I wanted to thank this Dr. Munch for his willingness to document the gas chamber operation, but this sounded strange, even to me! However, one morning I woke up with this idea: How about a letter of forgiveness, from me to Dr. Munch?

LEVEL 3—FORGIVENESS AS CHANNEL

What I discovered then was life-changing. I discovered that I had the power to forgive! No one could give me that power, no one could take it away; it was all mine to use in any way I wished. That was very interesting; because as a victim, for almost 50 years, I never thought that I had any power over my life. Writing that letter took over four months, but in the end, my English professor who corrected it said, "That's very nice, to forgive this Dr. Munch, but your problem is not with Dr. Munch, but with Dr. Mengele!"

I was not quite ready to forgive Dr. Mengele, but she said, "I've been correcting this letter; now I want you to do me a favor. When you go home tonight, pretend that Mengele is in the room, and you are telling him you forgive him. If you could do that, I would like to know: How would it make you feel?

Interesting idea! When I got home, I picked up a dictionary, and wrote down 20 nasty words, which I read, clear and loud, pretending that Mengele was in the room, and at the end I said: "In spite of all that, I forgive you!" It made me feel very good—that I, the little guinea pig for 50 years, had power over the Angel of Death of Auschwitz!

Dr. Munch and I arrived in Auschwitz, and I read my declaration of Amnesty, and signed it. Dr. Munch signed his document, and I felt free! Free from Auschwitz, free from Mengele. I know most of the survivors denounced me for doing this, but what is forgiveness? I like it; it's an act of self-healing, self-liberation, self-empowerment!

All victims who have been hurt feel hopeless, helpless, and powerless. Remember that we can't change what happened; that's the tragic part. But we can change how we relate to it.

CONSCIOUSNESS AT THE CHANNEL LEVEL

This level is all about realizing that there is a bigger purpose here than just human comfort or convenience. As Shakespeare wrote in *As You Like It*, "All the world's a stage, and all the men and women merely players." We are living out a divine drama, and we are playing a part in it. And we're not just playing the role. We are also the co-author.

You've given yourself permission to feel your feelings, vent them all and express them towards your perpetrator, verbally or in writing. You have moved into taking back control from that situation or person, reclaimed power over your life, and taken action to start changing your conditions. Now you are ready to step into becoming a conduit for a Higher Power. Not always and not forever, but you need *to begin* to perceive that there is a higher purpose unfolding in your life.

You begin to see situations not as having been done *to* you, but rather, that life is conspiring *for you*, by presenting difficulties to overcome. This is not easy to understand or accept, if the issue you're working on was deeply traumatic. You do not condone the wrong actions, but you are stepping into the first stage of a more transcendent model of life. If reading this brings up anger or resistance, go back to the first two stages and work through the feelings that come up, until you are ready for this stage. On the other hand, if you feel some resonance here, and you know that there is something more for you to discover, then continue.

There is a bigger picture

What's really going on in life is that there is a bigger pattern than just our individual life unfolding. We are part of a universal reality, like

LEVEL 3—FORGIVENESS AS CHANNEL

a gigantic play, with many characters playing their various parts. Some play the enemies, while others are our friends and allies. We have actually written our role before ever being born; but if we don't like it, we have the power to change it.

We can step back into our spiritual Self, the author of the play—and see ourselves as not just the character, but the actor in it, and not harmed at all by what is happening. We hold no blame, but only compassion for those who have the villain scripts; they say and do what is needed for us to play our part.

It's like what Judas did to Jesus; Jesus had an expanded consciousness and knew that Judas had to do what he did so that Jesus could also play his part in the grand scheme of things. Judas, on the human level, was betraying a friend, and that's why he hung himself. He was not able to reach the spiritual understanding to see that before they were ever born, he had agreed to play the part of the villain. If Judas had been able to see that deeper truth, he could have forgiven himself. But Jesus, with his expanded consciousness, saw it all, and thanked Judas for the kiss.

We now start to realize that we are an instrument endowed with free will through which God—Life, Truth, Universal Intelligence—acts in the world. We need to surrender to that energy. When we act from personal will, bad things can happen. But when we surrender our personal will of how things should be, of how we want them to be, and let go, then the divine will can manifest.

Here is where we recognize that the people who hurt us were not specifically trying to do so. They were just doing what was best for them, being the way they were conditioned to be. It's what they will do until they wake up to a higher idea of who they are; their behavior was scripted to allow us to expand our awareness of how things work. It's our choice to allow it or not.

If you've been betrayed, now you are ready to recognize that what caused this pain and hurt may have a grander purpose to it. You realize there's something bigger here than your ego's ideas of what should or shouldn't be. While still in the metaphysical, you are moving into the spiritual. Now that you have felt your feelings, claimed your power, taken control over conditions, and generated and created at a certain level, you are now ready to let go of some control and open up to the idea that there's something more here.

You decide that there's a lesson, there's a blessing, there's a growth opportunity. You surrender control and open up to a greater purpose, a greater potential to be manifested. You become a channel for something greater to express through you.

From the perspective of a divine drama going on, you know you've cast those people in your life to help you learn, to help you get stronger. Now you can forgive at a deeper level, letting go of all blame. You begin to feel gratitude for those experiences, and your thankfulness neutralizes the pain. Being grateful activates the blessing of awareness that there are ideas bigger than what's merely going on in our human experience—greater powers than ourselves, worldwide plans, greater purposes, and soul contracts—all of which you were not aware of before.

You can release the control you thought you had as creator of your reality to a Higher Power. You need some spiritual understanding to start on this journey. In ultimate Reality, everything is always working for your good, no matter how it appears. In the mind of God, there is no need to forgive anything, since there is no awareness of limitation or evil. Through the expanded consciousness of holding no blame, forgiveness is automatic, without having to invoke it.

In this stage, when we surrender to a Higher Power, instead of God being outside and far off, we realize that He is working through us. We are becoming a conduit for God to be expressed.

Integration of the levels

When we have truly integrated the beginning levels, then we have not only taken responsibility, but we begin to understand the higher spiritual purpose of our painful experiences. We see that we are channels for something much bigger than we first thought, and we are ready and willing to discover the deeper meaning, the blessing, and the reason for these things happening. They were catalysts for our greater awakening, freedom, and fulfillment.

As we continue working on our perceptions and on integrating the shifts, we finally realize that as long as we surrender to a power that we perceive as "outside," we are still separate. The ultimate goal is full integration with Spirit. We must transition from surrender to a "separate" God into the realization that we are not—and never have been—separate from God.

The four levels are just descriptions of our different states of mind; they are not real. Striving to integrate more of our spiritual Self is like trying to fill up a glass that's already full; it can't be done. We must integrate the physical sense of self into the spiritual Self. It's time to extricate ourselves from religious teachings that say we are a worm in the dust, and instead, accept our godliness.

In the later stages of this level, we realize that forgiveness now comes from a place of power, of knowing that the divinity we are identified with is speaking through us and can't be hurt in any way by the actions of people who have forgotten their divinity, and so, act in less than divine ways. It means that we forgive—not their actions, but the fact that they disowned their divinity.

We see it's the pain of separation that caused them to lash out at us, and our willingness to forgive is proof of our divine connection, which guides our actions. We can thank them for reminding us of what we came here to heal: the unconsciousness and the identification with a physical personality. When we forgive from spiritual consciousness, it has the potential of transforming them, since from the vantage point of Spirit, we see and acknowledge them as Divinity, too.

Eventually, we'll reach Level 4—Oneness—where we are no longer merely a Channel, but spiritual being itself. From this stage, however, it's very important that we don't rush into it, because there is great value in being a Channel. It must be fully integrated before the next step becomes available. Understand, this process is a lifelong endeavor—even many lifetimes long. Even spiritual masters do not reach full Level 4 consciousness permanently. It's periodic at best. Jesus sometimes spoke about God the Father, and other times from the I AM perspective—that is, from the Oneness of God.

Right now, we're just working on acknowledging that there's something bigger, which wants to express through us. We can forgive any situation by recognizing that other people have been playing a part, just like we have. They didn't do anything to actually hurt us. From this larger view of Reality, there was a soul contract made long ago. Someone else plays the bad guy, so that we can access and activate more of our heroic potential. Conflict is necessary in drama, just like it is in nature, for the activation and expression of more potential.

ASPECTS OF FORGIVENESS FROM THE CHANNEL LEVEL

Forgiving others

Back to our betrayal example again, at this level, you immediately realize that as painful as being betrayed by your partner is, you know there is a higher purpose to all of it, even if you don't know yet what that is. You feel a loosening of judgment and blame and hold no resentment, focusing on the life that can now unfold differently, because of that betrayal. You can look at your situation and ask: *What is it drawing out from me? Who do I need to become to transcend it, to be so strong that it can't touch me?*

LEVEL 3—FORGIVENESS AS CHANNEL

In this process, you bring to mind any earlier experience that was painful. How did that cause you to grow and develop? What were the benefits, gifts, lessons, and blessings? As you reflect, maybe you begin to see that the experience didn't really hurt you or take anything away in the ultimate sense. It helped create a condition for more of you to emerge.

When you look at yourself as the author of your script, you have given the actor—yourself—the freedom to choose how to interpret the script. Every other person in that play has the same freedom. You stop identifying as the character who suffers and blames others; you rise into the author role, who knows this is only a drama in the dimension of time and space, starting at a certain point and finishing at a given time—and then all the players go out and have a drink together.

The divine script is eternal perfection. Since that does not exist in this world, you realize that even what is called good is just a relative perception of a pattern of absolute perfection. What is good can become better—infinitely and eternally. You know you are a part of that larger pattern, and an instrument for it all to unfold. That divine pattern is perfect.

The pattern in the acorn is a pattern of a perfect oak, but depending on outer conditions, the tree may not unfold perfectly. For now, however, all you need to know is that there is a perfect pattern to life, and you are a channel for that. Forgiveness is a powerful tool for becoming a better instrument for that pattern to unfold, and ultimately to free you of any personalization of the people in your life. Instead, you realize they are a cast of characters with soul contracts—all conspiring together for the evolution of your soul and the unfoldment of your greater potential.

Therefore, at this level, forgiving others means having compassion, and seeing others' true nature regardless of the actions taken by their personalities.

A Tibetan monk was imprisoned and tortured for months by the Chinese, but in the end he managed to escape and make his way to the West. His story was reported to the Dalai Lama, who wished to hear about it first-hand. The monk came to him and recounted everything he had suffered, all the tortures he had undergone.

> *"In the end, I was really, really afraid—"*
> *"You were afraid of dying?" asked the Dalai Lama.*
> *"Oh no," said the monk, "that would have been a relief! I was really afraid of losing my compassion!"*

Self-forgiveness

Forgiving yourself for actual transgressions, for harming others, is the most difficult to achieve in Levels 1 and 2, where we are identifying with the material body. But as we move to a more transcendent perspective, we see that just as no one has ever truly or permanently harmed us, we haven't harmed anyone else. Like Judas and Jesus, we are each playing a part. We don't condone our bad behavior, but we make amends, apologize, restore what's been taken or lost, and so on. The point is, what's bad often creates a condition that leads to what's good or better. Then there might be up or down cycles, like we see in politics and in personal relationships.

The metaphysical teaching—that ultimately no harm has ever been done—is a very dangerous one unless we have reached a certain level of spiritual maturity, since it can easily be used as justification for harming others. This transcendent concept will actually harm us while we're in the levels of Victim or Creator. To fully understand this aspect, we must be in the latter part of Level 3, Channel consciousness.

As we're willing to see the person who has harmed us as a character in a play—where we are the hero or heroine of our life—likewise, when we are the person who has done harm, we need to step back and give ourselves similar understanding and compassion.

LEVEL 3—FORGIVENESS AS CHANNEL

It was for another's evolution that we did what we did, as well as for our own. But of course always make sure to remedy any harm caused.

We can start by forgiving ourselves for all the perceptions we have of good and bad. In the realm of duality, everything has been orchestrated for our ultimate success. Human experience is just a relative place on the spectrum of good/bad, where we find ourselves; but it never reaches the absolute spiritual wholeness and completeness we are striving to comprehend, where everything exists in a perfect nondual Reality.

Forgiving deceased people

Even when no longer here, people who have passed away were characters in your play. Now they have gone offstage. They still exist, even if you don't believe that. The only difference from when they were alive is that now you can't talk to them directly. So it's time to discover *What was the meaning of the part they played*? Ask *What has been the benefit, the gift they gave to me*? What was the author's intent in writing that script for the evolution of your soul and the activation of your greater potential? Discovering the answers will allow you to release them, and maybe even be grateful to them.

However, if you have any feeling other than lovingkindness towards them, you are temporarily back in Level 1 or 2. Go back and do more forgiveness work on that, as explained in Chapters 7 and 8.

Soul contracts

Some people can be viewed as actors under contract to play certain parts in the drama you imagined as the author of the play you are living. They either have fulfilled it, or they are fulfilling it now. But it's just a concept that lives at this transformational paradigm of reality. You must become the solution for every trigger, for every problem you encounter with anyone. It must be done within yourself, because you are the author, director, actor, and character in the play of your life.

> ## Meditation Exercise
>
> Try sitting in meditation. From the place of knowing that you've set up this scenario for your own advancement, imagine asking the troubling people in your life (even those who have passed on): *What would you say to me now, to lessen my pain?* Tell them that you want to truly understand how this is helping you grow.
>
> Imagine the words you would like to hear, and repeat them to your heart, over and over, for a minute or two at a time, many times throughout the day. Perhaps they answer, *You wanted to experience patience* (or love, or courage) *and I loved you enough to give you the opportunity!* Put your hand over your heart if it's helpful to feel their love for you. Your mantra is like a magnet that attracts all of the unresolved concepts out of your body, so that you can become the resolution that they cannot be.
>
> This journey is about your consciousness, your expansion, and your willingness to be for yourself what no one else is guaranteed to be for you.

Forgiving God

Forgiving God at this level is about recognizing God as the ultimate divine author and stage manager who is helping to create the setup

LEVEL 3—FORGIVENESS AS CHANNEL

and the scenery for you to live out this divine drama, so that you can become the best hero or heroine of your own life. So you could ask God *What are you trying to teach me through this?* or *What do you want me to become because of this?*

Your concept of God now is completely different from when you had full permission to be angry at God in Level 1, and taking back your power from God in Level 2. Forgiveness at this stage is not something we do, but what naturally happens as a by-product of the work we do and the insights we have when we realize that life is all a play. We see there really isn't anything to forgive, so the word *forgive* isn't even in the vocabulary of late Level 3 and Level 4.

Maybe by now you're thinking that there is nothing to forgive God for, since it's all been orchestrated with a purpose—and that's exactly right! However, if you don't really feel that way, if instead you feel hurt, pain, fear, or anger, that's great, too—more opportunities to heal.

I want to be very clear about one thing: When I say "forgiving God" here, what's actually happening now looks very different from any previous concept of forgiveness. In fact, when you're truly living at this level, forgiveness as we've known it no longer exists. You will know when a need for the lower levels of forgiveness occurs, because certain symptoms will show up. That's perfectly okay; it just means the work you're doing is effective, so more stuff is emerging to be healed. Go back, and go through the processes and exercises and do the forgiveness work at Levels 1 and 2 again. That's progress!

When no more symptoms occur, there is such a thing as *living in a state of forgiveness*. That means that forgiveness is not attached to any object, person, or group. You simply forgive anything that comes into your awareness because it's only a relative expression of the infinite perfection of Source energy.

WHY WE STAY AT CHANNEL LEVEL

When we can't forgive, we are holding on to resentment and blame, and perpetuating our disconnection from God and from every other expression of God. As long as we keep a sense of a self separate from God—a self that can be wounded, betrayed, or in any way diminished—we are not yet One with God.

Let's go back to the example of being betrayed. We have forgiven on many levels, so we can actually see how this occurrence has helped us grow to the point of allowing Spirit to be expressed through us. We see progress in our ways of responding to circumstances, and we have peace of mind, even if unwelcome things still happen.

We can recognize that the energy of unhappiness was stuck inside and just wanted to move. Think about it: an *e-motion* is a "moving out"—*energy in motion*. We have evolved in this stage to a place where that can safely happen. We consciously release our emotions with an effective focus on *how we want to feel*.

But perhaps with so much good in our life, there is also a tendency to hold on to what we have, and metaphorically to rest on our laurels. We don't go out and try something new, because we don't want to put ourselves at risk of failing. So, in order to continue to progress, we have to be shaken out of complacency and stagnation. This usually happens because of a crisis. That's why bad things happen to good people: to move them into a more expanded consciousness. We could progress without crises, but human nature being what it is, that is usually not the case.

And so, even while in many ways we feel empowered at this point, we know we were betrayed—just when we thought bad things couldn't happen anymore! Here, there may be more at stake than just our personal evolution. Let's look at the example of Nelson Mandela. He was in prison for 27 years, where he could have become

LEVEL 3—FORGIVENESS AS CHANNEL

bitter and resentful, but instead, he chose to be a better version of himself. He forgave the authorities and his jailers, and he came out to free his entire country from apartheid, peacefully and without resentment towards anyone. Until the very end, Nelson Mandela was unaware of what his real purpose was. All he knew was that he wanted freedom for his people. He didn't know whether he would ever succeed. But he was willing to put his own freedom and his life on the line for his convictions.

In the same way you—who in this case have been betrayed by your partner—are not aware of the bigger implications of that situation. But if you keep your focus on the Divinity within you, and only take the steps you imagine your soul would take, you become the Channel for your soul's purpose to manifest. Then, the ultimate outcome can be only good. Maybe you'll find that the relationship was keeping you from reflecting on your soul's purpose for this lifetime. Perhaps having a family to look after as well as keeping a job to have financial security would have never given you the possibility to invest yourself in the highest purpose your soul planned for you, even if right now you have no idea what it is. But your life will now unfold differently.

Consider the biblical story of Joseph (see Genesis chapter 37–47). He was sold into slavery by his brothers, then wrongly accused of misdemeanors and imprisoned. But many years later, he became the second-most powerful man in the kingdom, and he ended up being able to save all the people from famine—including his brothers, whom he forgave.

Potentially, neither the freeing of South Africa from apartheid nor the saving of the Egyptian and Jewish people from famine could have happened without those bad things happening to those individuals. Had they known the higher purpose, it would have made their hardships easier to endure; but whether they knew it or not, the divine purpose would eventually manifest. If either of them had refused to grow, to become better and so (unknowingly) further the divine plan, Source would have found another soul willing and able to do that. We, as personalities, do not have the power to thwart the divine plan; however, we can choose to prevent it from happening through us. In that case, we end up living in suffering, without a glimmer of light to sustain us through the hardships.

THE PROCESS FOR MOVING TO THE NEXT LEVEL

We have now seen how to forgive humanly from the Victim, Creator, and Channel Levels. We have realized the relative nature of everything in the material world, where good things can lead to bad and vice versa. If we say I finally got this job I wanted! God must be looking after me! but then that leads to some terrible thing happening to us, it's just like the Zen parable:

> *A farmer and his son are working on the farm with their horse, but the horse gets loose and runs away.*
>
> *Their neighbor comes to commiserate, "Oh, you have bad fortune! Look at that: Your only horse is gone now!" The farmer says, "Maybe so; maybe not!"*
>
> *The horse comes back the next day, bringing a herd of wild mustangs, and now the farmer has a dozen horses instead of one. The neighbor says: "Good fortune has shined upon you! You have all these horses!" The farmer replies: "Maybe so; maybe not!"*
>
> *Then his son is out there with the horses, and he gets trampled and breaks his leg. The neighbor comes again to say, "Indeed you have bad luck!" and the farmer says: "Maybe so; maybe not!"*
>
> *Then war erupts in the kingdom, and soldiers come and recruit all the young men to fight the enemy, but because the farmer's son has a broken leg, he doesn't get taken. All the men who went from that village die in the war and never come back. Then the*

LEVEL 3—FORGIVENESS AS CHANNEL

neighbor says: "Truly, good fortune has befallen you, for your son has been spared!" The farmer says: "Maybe so; maybe not!"

And the story goes on and on like that, showing that the wise farmer is holding all experience and opinions and positions very lightly. He's more anchored in the universal principle that there is indeed an ultimate good, yet you can't merely look at appearances and determine what's good or bad.

Less and less forgiveness is necessary as we move into the deep understanding that even our misfortunes and transgressions serve a divine purpose of growth to the next stage of our development, if we are willing to learn. On a spiritual level, the material reality does not exist. Even what we call a healing is just material good, a relative expression of the underlying absolute spiritual goodness.

In this Channel Level we come to realize that our life, from the time we are born, has been just like having a bad dream—where we are drowning and crying out for help to the people on the shore, but no one seems to hear. Finally, people point to where we are struggling, but they don't come to the rescue. They are afraid of the big waves washing over us. Now we're short of breath, exhausted and we feel like we're drowning. We ask: *Why did no one rescue me?* With that thought we wake up, still terrified and short of breath, but slowly we realize we are in bed, safe and sound, and that it was all a dream; those people who left us to drown don't really exist. When we wake up, do we have to forgive those people? Of course not. They were never real, no matter how much we felt abandoned and betrayed. There never was any danger, even if we experienced the fear and the resentment.

We are now waking up to our genuine, spiritual life—where all the pain and suffering we experienced in our human life isn't even real.

Now, when we see anger, hate, violence, anxiety, and so on being expressed by anyone—whether it's personal or in the news—it's our job to silently send them thoughts of compassion, peace, harmony, and abundance. Here is where we become a catalyst for change in our environment, as well as for any people who come into our consciousness. We are called to send them whatever is needed, because we can see that they have forgotten that they are a part of Source energy—which is absolute Love. A positive energy is more powerful than a negative one; it will stay in their field until they are able to open up to it. This may not always be immediate, but I have seen it operate instantly.

> ### Blessing Exercise
>
> Here's what you can do in a situation where you have no power or possibility of changing it: Instead of going into fear, blame, or rejection, remember that you are a Channel—a conduit through which God acts—and bless the person with the opposite quality.
>
> When you see abuse, say in your heart *May you be blessed with kindness*!
> When it's betrayal, say in your heart *May you be blessed with faithfulness*!
> When it's stealing, say in your heart *May you be blessed with abundance*!
> When it's disrespect, say in your heart *May you be validated*!
> You can also think back to your childhood, make a list of all those who have upset, wronged, or hurt you in any way. If there is still some pain or distress about a situation, take time, every day, just as you take a shower every day, to stand under the shower of your forgiveness, washing away the dirt and grit of the journey, by saying:
> *I forgive everyone for everything, everywhere, forever—including myself.*

LEVEL 3—FORGIVENESS AS CHANNEL

> If that doesn't feel authentic, if there is any resistance, then try this first:
> *God, the Divine, help me to forgive everyone for everything, everywhere, forever—including myself.*
> That you can probably do; so then try the next level:
> *I am willing to forgive everyone for everything, everywhere, forever—including myself.*
> Keep this one up until you feel it's real for you, and then take the final step:
> *I forgive everyone for everything, everywhere, in every way—including myself!*
> Make this a daily practice. Really feel your words, and notice how meaning them becomes easier over time. As you get to compassion for each person, cross them off your list; you're no longer their victim.
> As a way of healing the world, you can continue with a daily, final blessing: *May all people and all beings be blessed with love, peace, justice, compassion, abundance and joy forever.*

When we have spiritually awakened, we still see harm being done at the material level, but we are also aware of the good it produces. For instance, atrocities committed in the Middle East generate a wave of compassion and willingness to help: Doctors and psychologists go out to assist; organizations bring food and clothing, books, and toys for children; people are donating financially; they are praying and anchoring positive energy. People are giving what they are able to give—which is the real meaning of forgiveness. We are *for-giving*, not *for-taking*, or *for-attacking*, or *for-killing*.

Being a Channel for divine energy makes us more and more willing to truly take action on the material, ground level to change unacceptable conditions—to feed the hungry, give to the poor, protect the abused. We do our part in whatever way we can to actually improve the way things are—right where we are—as well as doing the spiritual work.

To fully integrate this level is a lifelong adventure. Start wherever you are. Wherever you are is the perfect place for you to be in order to take the next step on the journey. That said, I caution you not to get too spiritually ambitious, not to compare yourself to others, and not to let the ego make you wrong for not being "there" yet.

We need to embody every small step, incrementally, to become a better and stronger channel for the Divine.

Review

Now, let me lay out a quick summary of the first three levels, because taken together, they form a dynamic sequence that you can run every hurt through, whether personal or global. (We will be discussing global issues in Chapter 11.) They also prepare you to step into Level 4, our next chapter, which is about your spiritual growth into being One with the Power of Source.

The first Level, Victim, is about really feeling the feelings brought up by the event, getting clear on what we want, taking some kind of productive action towards valuing ourselves, and filling ourselves back up again with appreciation. Then we express our feelings to the perpetrator in the strongest way, as a letter that we never send. (All of this can also be applied to global wrongs.)

The second Level, Creator, is about taking back our power and control over conditions. That's where we now take specific actions, create new habits, and design a life that is based on the idea of how we would show up if we had power and control again.

Then in Level 3, Channel, we are able to recognize that our problems may have a deeper meaning and a different purpose from what we first thought. We see that they were a catalyst for our spiritual growth, which we wouldn't have achieved without the trauma and the pain.

CHAPTER 10

LEVEL 4—FORGIVENESS FROM ONENESS

The weak can never forgive. Forgiveness is the attribute of the strong.
—Mahatma Gandhi

Before saying anything else, I want to make it quite clear that in my experience, this stage is very rarely achieved, at least consistently—even by people we call masters. So I have no way of speaking about this level from a place of personal knowledge. It's more a conceptual and research-based exploration. Since we are all unique, our concepts and experiences will be absolutely unique, too.

If you don't resonate with the ideas given here, it's perfectly all right; but consistently practicing forgiveness will help accelerate the process of rising ever-higher—and isn't that what you really wanted to achieve by reading this book?

This chapter is about spiritual growth and awakening to the mystical path, where the only goal is Oneness with Ultimate Reality. It's no longer really about forgiveness, as it can't even exist at this level. We work the other three levels again and again to purify our consciousness, and then the sense of a separate self just falls away. Like when we release weights from a hot air balloon and it rises, we naturally ascend to this stage—where all desire for anything falls away, leaving only the realization of Oneness and Truth.

Our only prayer becomes *God, more than anything, I want to wake up to the Truth that makes me free. I want to be an instrument of love, a conduit of peace on the planet. Open my eyes and my heart, show me what You want me to see, teach me what You want me to know, tell me what You want me to hear, give me what You want me to have, so I may be an embodiment of Truth and fulfill my true destiny and purpose.*

Once we are on this mystical path, there are no forgiveness techniques. If anything comes up that needs forgiveness, we go back to Levels 1, 2 and 3 for the issue, and when it's done, we return to the love of God, Truth, and renewed desire for a realization of Oneness. When more stuff comes up, it's always a signal that there is still a part of our consciousness at a lower level, so we have to deal with that at the lower stages first before getting back to the higher level.

Eventually, our personal work gets completed, and we experience a deeper mystical space of Union. Then we become a channel for dealing with society or global issues, and on and on it goes! This is the final stage as a human being, where you have to let go of any vestige of a belief of you as distinct from God. Here, the word *forgiveness* no longer applies; it no longer has the same meaning as before. Because God is you and you are God. And there is no principle about forgiving, because *evil* and *lack* don't exist, so the work you do at this level becomes about realizing the inherent positive quality of what you used to consider to be evil.

It's a shift in consciousness to perceive as God perceives. We see souls, rather than human beings. We realize only I AM—because ultimately there is no self other than God, so there is actually nobody to forgive. All the trials and tribulations we went through at the previous levels were real at the relative level, but as we rise into the absolute, we realize there is only wholeness, perfection, and Oneness. You were the actor playing all the parts, and there was never anyone actually hurt, neither was there anyone who did the hurting.

Ideally, our actions stem from that knowing. When they don't, we have come out of Oneness back into one of the other three levels.

Initially, we get only little glimpses of that stage. Pure bliss. No sense of a self separate from anything else, because *there is nothing else*. We are lost in just being, without thought, feeling, or doing—as if all experiences were just a story that never really happened. With practice, these moments will get longer.

As long as we have life, we have to come back to a more engaged state, or we could not function in this world. We remember those transcendent moments and experiences when we pierce the veil and have a moment of Oneness. The story of being human falls away, as if it had never been. Those moments are the only true Reality that exists. It's our actual soul existence before having a body. I believe it's what Jesus meant by the phrase "before Abraham was, I am" (John 8:58). It's as if Jesus were standing behind the entire veil of human existence, and with that one statement, all the karma of the world was erased; in an instant, we can be free of it all. Because I am before Abraham. Before my name and your name, I AM. Before this life experience, I AM.

That means that the I AM which we have just glimpsed pre-exists all human experience, and is here now, and will always be—holding within Itself the whole sphere of human time-and-space experience.

Achieving Oneness

As spiritual teacher Matt Kahn pointed out, the capital I also stands for the Roman numeral one (I). So I and 1 (I) are indistinguishable. We are One—before we ever even came into being.

Another thing to notice is that all problems exist only within time. The reason for that is because we need time to have a story—to have a problem. Karma is just a pattern that exists in the dimensions of time and space. That means that when we get out of time—out of the tenses of past, present, and future—and into the *now*, we touch the dimension of ourselves that has no story, no karma, no problems, no beginning, and no end. The patterns of cause and effect that are playing out as the stories in our life are erased. This is what it means to rise above the law of cause and effect into a Life of Grace, where you are free from sin—from error—and you're available to all the good of life, without having to earn or achieve anything.

Oneness is achieved from the physical plane and happens through embodying divine consciousness. In this Union, we are in a dimension outside of time and space, which is just a measurement of unfoldment. That's where each of us truly exists. From that vantage point where nothing material exists, no evil exists, and where no harm has ever been done, life is just a story passing before you, which never actually touches you. When you live in that "secret place of the Most High" (Psalm 91:1), in the place of Oneness with God, you come to realize that you have never left the Kingdom of Heaven. Believing you were separate from God was all a mistake. The truth is, you actually emanate from God, to bring your unique expression of Divinity into the Earth plane.

Try to remember our example of the person who betrayed you—when your consciousness was at a lower level—and go back to your own experience where you needed to forgive. After all this inner work, all you feel now is love for the unique expressions of God that these individuals are. They are embodiments of Love, being projected onto everyone in their life, to further everyone's growth. Maybe you don't even perceive them as separate in any way from the being that you are. All those things which you thought happened have no reality for you any longer. They are like a dream. And now you're awake.

LEVEL 4—FORGIVENESS FROM ONENESS

LIVING IN THIS CONSCIOUSNESS

Any experience of being in Oneness is subjective, and must necessarily be different for each person. There is at least a progression.

Beginning level: At this level, we have a realization that we are not only the character in the play or dream called Life, but also the actor and the author of it. We are the One Being, one nature, one Love—and so is everyone else; therefore, there is only One, and that One can never harm Itself, so no forgiveness is necessary.

As long as we are conscious of being *a specific expression* of the Divine, and *surrendering* to God—we are still split, not yet in complete Oneness. However, we do begin to identify more with our changeless divine Self. We're also aware that as long as we are alive, we dwell on the relative level of experience.

Later level: We start by forgiving the original perception that we're separate from God, and then we realize that even *that* needs no forgiveness, since it was the will of God to express Itself in physicality and to allow the journey of forgetfulness and reuniting with Source by free choice. Notice that we are not reuniting with God—from God's viewpoint—because God has no awareness that there was ever any division. It's simply the mechanism of God's infinite unfoldment in time and space, as form. Contrast, challenge, and polarity allow us to keep discovering and expressing more of our infinite nature.

We are not on our way back *to* anything, not even to God. We are radiating *from* the Source of All Life—from wholeness, completeness, and perfection—and starting to express more and more of that infinite nature. Therefore we forgive whatever comes our way—good or bad, whether we like it or dislike it, agree or disagree with it—we just forgive everything that appears, because it is simply a finite form, not the *is*ness of infinity.

In complete Oneness consciousness, there is no question of anything needing to be forgiven, because everything is part of the one divine energy. While we experience lack, limitation, problems, or evil on the human level, we realize that *that* whole level is an illusion, in which most people are lost. We know and live in the *spiritual* Reality, where there is nothing wrong. We acknowledge the temporary illusion, but we are not *of* it.

It's like seeing what appears to be the edge of the Earth on the horizon; but we know that's an optical illusion. We see what appears to be water on a desert highway, but we know that it's an optical illusion created by heat waves. We don't stop and wait for the water to dry up; we don't pray to remove it; we see the mirage for what it is and keep driving.

Having a body is a gift

As long as we are alive, we can't break away from being both human and divine. We aspire to stay at the level of Oneness, but very few of us, if any, achieve it permanently. We get fleeting glimpses of it, but the finite human mind is not able to grasp infinity and eternity, so we have to be open to perceiving it without trying to hold onto it. It's just like putting your hand in a river to try and hold the water flowing past. It can't be done by closing your hand on it—there's nothing in your hand. But if you open your hand, you feel the whole of the river flowing, and you experience it all.

The same is true for our experience of Oneness. As soon as we try to understand the experience, know something about it, and hold onto the feeling we have, it recedes, because as soon as we know or feel or think something about it, we have objectified it—made it into an object that we own. It becomes our thoughts and our feelings. But Consciousness can't be objectified or owned; it's a container that holds everything material, including our thoughts and feelings,

LEVEL 4—FORGIVENESS FROM ONENESS

within Itself. Here's where we see that truly we are not *in* the world; the whole world is *in us*.

Progression of awareness

In our beginning stage as a newborn, and in the first 6 to 12 months, we were still in union with Spirit. I believe this time of early childhood closely resembles the Oneness stage that we can get glimpses of later in life, whenever we expand our awareness. But it's not the same experience. As a child, what we have is a memory of that State of Oneness, a condition which we had to leave through the fact of being born—which we later must reclaim through consciously deciding it.

At conception, the Infinite Spirit incarnates into a fetus, and it is the animating principle of the baby's growth. But after birth, we gradually lose the memory of being in Spirit, because we are now bound by a material sense of a body. We have to learn to live in this different dimension. As the body grows, the mind and awareness expand, and we are able to reach back into the Spirit we always had—if we want it and choose it.

Where we really live is outside of time and space, outside a material expression. We know that, because when life decides to withdraw from the body, our body can no longer see, or hear, or do anything. So from the point of view of the spiritual Self, our temporal life is just a concept in the Mind of God.

GOING BEYOND FORGIVENESS

From this level, where we realize no harm or hurt has ever been done and nothing was lost, forgiveness will not look as it did at the lower levels. If forgiveness is truly and deeply embraced, it can lead to dropping all need to even hold people accountable, often resulting in a healing, and the return of what appeared to have been lost.

On the other hand, it can also lead to holding people accountable in more powerful ways. Jesus did not mince his words when speaking to the Pharisees and priests. Jesus brought the sword of Truth when he preached; he came to "turn a man against his father, a daughter against her mother" (see Matthew 10:35). Jesus afflicted the comfortable, as many other masters have done.

Life is a divine play

At level 4, we can see life on Earth as a divine drama where all situations conspire for the ultimate freedom and fulfillment of the hero. Every character is a soul we made a contract with, to accelerate our evolution. We are all playing parts, and when the curtain falls, we'll go off and have a drink together, have a laugh, and talk about this amazing play we were in.

In the beginning of Oneness consciousness we realize we are the actor, not the character; we are involved, but never lost in the drama. We are someone outside of this play, and the character we are playing—who got betrayed or killed—has no actual reality, no actual life, even if it appears solid and present. That character is just a concept, as is the character who betrayed or killed us, and we have no hard feelings against the actor whose character harmed our character—since neither really exists.

Identifying with the actor who knows the outcome of the play allows us to realize we are also the author—so that the character can grow and evolve and finally slay the dragon and win the princess. The actor would never think *I really need to do some forgiveness work on what you did to me in Act Two. I'm really upset about that.* None of this affects us in any way, because we know every trial imagined for the character will get the character closer to the end of the play where

LEVEL 4—FORGIVENESS FROM ONENESS

the character is triumphant. The author knows no harm can ever come to the actors, because they have never left the spiritual Reality.

The grand play was the illusion all characters had, which is the story of Adam and Eve in the Bible. They ate of the fruit that symbolized the knowledge of good and evil. Before that, all they knew was good (see Genesis Chapter 23). Another point to consider is that at the start of the story when "a deep sleep" falls upon Adam—so that God could create Eve from his rib—nowhere in that story do we ever hear that he woke up! Everything after that is a part of the dream—the illusion of duality, of time and space, of good and bad. They had to keep on living in that illusion, until they could come back into knowing the eternal Truth of Only Good. We are now waking up to that Truth.

As we continue letting go of our sense of ourselves as a character, separate from God, we now realize only I AM—and we no longer even need to say *I am that I AM*. There is no more God "out there" to forgive or to look up to, and no Self other than God. The situation we are experiencing is actually part of a larger plan and purpose, to make us more awake and aware of ultimate Reality.

There is only good

Simply put, in this final stage there can be no forgiveness, just as there can be no compassion in God's Mind. God does not see evil; if He did, it would be permanent. So when we tap into God's vision, we no longer see evil. Those concepts are beautiful human interpretations of how to extend love and allowance to our fellow man. When we see any error or lack, we are seeing from the level of the physical self; but now we understand we are not our physical self. Situations that victimized us were really painful; but after gaining the insights, wisdom, and healing from the earlier stages, those situations now hold the potential of even bigger insights about the nature of life, and the nature of the Self. A greater vision of ultimate enlightenment is unfolding.

Because of the principle of Oneness, if we identify anyone as a physical reality, we identify ourselves as that, too. We can't stay in Oneness unless we see all people as the perfect spiritual beings they have always been.

Having done all this work, with the insights we've received, we get to see that this was not a journey simply about forgiving. Forgiveness was just a tool—one of many we could have used for reaching enlightenment. That's a very powerful realization. We understand that forgiveness is so much more than we ever thought it was. It opens the door wide to new levels and aspects of the journey of life.

Whenever we go far enough into any quality, at the deepest level we discover Love. We have discovered certain aspects of love in the lower levels of forgiving, and now we are beginning to love from the level of Love Itself—since God, Life, Light, and Love are all synonymous.

In the I AM consciousness, as opposed to *I am this* or *I am that*, there is nothing to forgive—either yourself, or others—since you are one with them, one with God, completely outside of duality. Forgiveness is necessary only at the lower levels of consciousness. Here, there is only God, expressed as Love. Anything else is a judgment, however good it seems on the human level.

We must abandon the concept of there being good vs. bad, of polarity of any sort. Polarity exists only in the relative realm. We have to go beyond the idea that a person being healed is good, and having a disease is bad. That's true in the human—relative—dimension; but we must go beyond that. We realize only spiritual Reality—that there is only wholeness and completeness beyond any possibility of there ever being disease, lack, or limitation. Beyond the good-or-bad appearance of health or wealth is the absolute expression of Divinity.

LEVEL 4—FORGIVENESS FROM ONENESS

The more we are anchored in that nondual Reality, the less we'll be on the roller-coaster of life in a physical plane.

While alive in the human realm, we necessarily vacillate between the I AM level and the physical level. We look at the human forms having experiences, at the level where we're called by our names and we're acting as personalities in time and space—but we also know that there is only Oneness. We are both.

There are not different dimensions of God as we go through these levels of consciousness, even if it seems like it. It's just our awareness of God—of Life, of the Universe, of Power that is evolving. As we realize that God is not outside of us, but we are It, then we are not coming from an ego place, but from an actual realized place of enlightened consciousness—where God is using us for the greater expression of Itself.

Oneness is a realm of absolutes. Joy is complete and perfect, so sadness doesn't exist. Harmony is complete and perfect, so that equates with no discord. Perfect peace means no conflict. Complete abundance is equal to no lack.

Practicing Non-attachment

All our attempts to better a human condition—whether it's in our body, our affairs, or in the world—are still coming from a place of separation, and therefore belong to the other three levels of consciousness. They have nothing to do with spirituality—that is, seeing with the eyes of God. In Oneness there is no principle about turning bad into good, since bad doesn't exist; there is no principle about turning poverty into wealth, sadness into happiness, sickness into health, or enemies into allies, because there isn't any sense of any duality in the mind of God. The spiritual realm is eternally whole and perfect.

Even in our best attempts to be good and spiritual people, even when we abandon the idea of resisting evil, and defying negativity, we're still attached to the good. That's an even harder obstacle to overcome—letting go of our desire for abundance, our desire to turn our body into a healthy one. Even if it's not easy to apprehend, being in Oneness means absolving not only transgressions, but letting go in all those places where we desire things, or don't want to lose what we have. Even wanting a better connection with Spirit is senseless. How can we want that, when we already have it? Do we desire that connection, or do we desire knowing and feeling that connection? Can we be content with not only being connected, but simply being One, and even letting go of the desire to feel it?

Our connection to God is unbreakable. We are no more or less connected to God when we feel it, or when we don't feel it. Nevertheless, remember what Jesus taught: "You shall know the truth, and the truth shall make you free" (John 8:32). It's our conscious knowing that allows us to experience more of the Infinite Truth. It's already here, but it is the *knowing* of it—not just intellectually, but directly—that makes it a part of our conscious awareness, and thus of our experience.

To the extent that we're attached even to the good, to that extent, we're still on the wheel of karma. Until we completely forgive everything, and come to the realization that there is only one Reality, then we'll no longer have the desire to change anything, fix anything, or manipulate conditions to our advantage. As long we have a material and personal sense of life—wanting to get something or get rid of something—it will manifest.

We are creators of what is in our consciousness! Consciousness always clothes itself in form; so, that material, personal sense will keep manifesting as personal and material existence. That's the cause of reincarnation. And there is nothing wrong with that; it is Law that as Creators, we manifest our perceptions. But we can choose to have a different perception, and then express the Divinity we are in other ways—now coming from a place of freedom. The purest, Ultimate State of Being is not resisting anything, not wanting anything—just being an open space for God to express all of Itself through us. It is like being the branch of a tree: The branch doesn't have to desire anything, because the tree is uniquely made manifest, by creating and caring for its branches.

It's not easy. We're mostly focused on stopping the cycle of violence; and that's necessary and great, at the level of our collective evolution. But we hardly ever hear about stopping the cycle of good as well—stopping the whole cycle of material perception—yet that's equally vital. We could be stopping the cycles of both evil and good simultaneously; but until our collective consciousness has risen enough to see what it means to be truly liberated as a transparency for Divinity, stopping violence will continue to be necessary. We need to realize that violence would no longer exist if we all dropped wanting stuff, holding on to what we've got, and resisting what is. We need to become a beholder of how the glory of God manifests through Its every expression.

How to advance into Oneness

When there is a real need to forgive, then you have a choice to make. People have made mistakes, and so have you. You can hold them at the level of their guilt and identify them according to the human drama of their guilt and error, in which case you are keeping yourself at the same human level of experiencing the results of your errors. Or, you can become willing to see the situation differently. You can turn to the spiritual aspect of yourself with a sincere prayer, and ask for help from your Divinity to extend your perception beyond what your physical senses perceive, to what your heart knows to be true: that they are a part of Divinity, exactly as you are. You become willing to give up focusing on their guilt, and instead see them as expressing the perfect life of Source.

Their guilt comes from their material self. They made a mistake, but beyond their physical self is the Truth of who they really are.

Now, if you are willing to release them and hold no judgment, then you are automatically set free, because spiritually, there is only One here. And that's the meaning behind the scriptural phrase, God's "only begotten son" (see John 3:16, 18 and 1 John 4:9): We are, each of us, the only begotten beloved child of God.

When you give up focusing on other people's guilt, you must also give up focusing on the past, because forgiveness can only happen in the present. If you are angry with them, it's because of something they did before this moment. If you are seeing them through the mental filter of their guilt, it means you're seeing them through the past—and the past does not exist, except in your memory. The past is just a concept—not a reality. The present moment is the only moment where God's time and human time are merged.

In human time, there might be something that needs to be done. Depending on what they did, there might be some accountability called for. But that will then be guided from a different place in consciousness, from *the now moment*, or God's perception. Everything we do is always infused with the consciousness with which we do it. When we take action from the standpoint of God's perception, the result must of necessity be beneficial and useful. While anything we do that's instilled with the consciousness of attack, revenge, or even defensiveness, will only continue the cycle of suffering.

Remember to make Divinity your primary relationship in every relationship you have. If you do that, all your relationships will fall into alignment. So first, we must accept our Oneness with the Divine. The ego is always pointing the finger of blame and looking for guilt, choosing to remember what's bad, what's not working.

Forgiveness, on the other hand, is also selective remembering—remembering the good, remembering that the love people gave you was real, the love you gave them was real; and that everything else is just a nightmare you're having. You can wake up, forget the nightmare and move on with your life, choosing anew.

CHAPTER 11

RADICAL FORGIVENESS THAT HEALS THE WORLD

A stunning lesson in forgiveness:

>Meena was happily married with two lovely children, but at one point, she felt she could no longer stay in the relationship and contacted a lawyer, despite strong opposition from her husband. A health problem sent her to a clinic, and she asked the lawyer to make sure the divorce papers would not arrive at her home while she was absent. The lawyer promised; however, the day she entered the clinic, the papers arrived, and her husband tried in vain to reach her by phone.
>
>That night, he turned on the kitchen gas and committed suicide, taking their two children along with him. Later the same night, the electricity, which had been disconnected in the whole region, was put on again. A spark created an explosion in the gas-filled house, and everything burned down.
>
>In one night, Meena lost her beloved children, her husband, and absolutely everything she owned on earth—everything.
>
>In her own words: "I had no religion to which I could cling, no therapist who could empathize with the violence of my

suffering. I had only the solitude of my suffering, crumbling inner defenses, and a bewildered ego which was falling to pieces."

Meena embarked on a seven-year journey of inner and outer exploration, travelling all over the world in her stubborn search for answers. And in Benares, India, facing the cremation fires along the river Ganges, she suddenly realized that the bodies she saw were only carcasses emptied of their essence and soul.

In that instant, she understood everything. Her children and their father had been the catalysts of her inner awakening—*"the miracle of grace was descending into my heart; my living faith without dogmas or belongingness; it was a spiritual awakening."* She experienced what forgiveness is really all about: It's a discovery of the gift that is hidden behind the trial—taking back the responsibility of what is happening to us, without any accusations towards people or the outside world.

The ultimate moment of forgiveness happened for Meena when she organized a simple ritual with her close friends in homage to her children and their father. At one moment, facing the portrait of the man with whom she had shared the best and the worst in her life, looking deep into his eyes, she suddenly understood that there had never been victims or a perpetrator—only soul contracts that had been accepted by all before coming to earth. Rivers of tears were transformed into gratitude. It was as if she remembered this past contract.

At that moment, a friend of hers in the room who is a medium said to Meena: "I have a message from Robert. He says: 'Finally you have understood! You remember. Thank you.'"

Then, added Meena, "I have this vision of his face, which has become so luminous, and of the children in the background, smiling and saying, 'We came to advance you on your spiritual path, as agreed upon.'"

For Meena, that was the ultimate gift. True forgiveness. And she concluded by saying, "What is there to add but gratitude."

RADICAL FORGIVENESS

Most people don't realize that they are not in the world, but that the whole world is in their consciousness. And so, wherever there's a trigger, a projection, some anger, fear, hate, shame, or guilt towards anyone or any situation, there is a pocket that needs forgiveness. This is where we move away from forgiving personal wrongs, because most people don't go beyond personal relationships when they think of forgiveness.

Here is where we start thinking globally of the human race — of forgiving historical incidences and issues, cultural stigmas, religious scars, and political leaders. Forgiving becomes a way of life, a way of meeting all those places where there is upset, fear, or sadness outside of our personal life. When people are triggered by Donald Trump, they don't think they need to forgive that projection within themselves or to forgive the things he does. Forgiving harm done by groups or to groups — based on race, culture, religion, gender, and so on — is not often thought of as needing forgiveness. We are usually simply horrified; but forgiveness in these instances is just as necessary.

Group forgiveness

From Victim Level, we are totally invested in what's happening relative to us personally. But if there is a group that a person is a part of — such as the military, a religion, race, culture, or gender — there may be global wounds that need forgiving as well. Has a particular incident caused us to think that men can't ever be trusted? Or that all women are capricious, unpredictable, and only concerned with their own well-being? It's time to heal that area of our beliefs. We'll need to forgive all men or all women.

From Creator Level, we forgive because it's a control game, because we're more conscious than others. We have authority, so we create a way of life that allows us to feel in charge of things and in charge of how we feel. Every time a negative thought arises, it's replaced with a positive one. We try to forgive anything upsetting that comes into our awareness because we don't like the way it makes us feel.

Anything that brings up animosity, fear, anger, or shame—such as wars, genocide, past or present triggering events—needs to be forgiven. For example, if your ex was of a different nationality, a different religion, or a different ethnic group, is there now distrust, resentment, or anger towards that entire group? Unless that's healed, it leads to some extreme behaviors, such as what we are witnessing in the world—the torturing and killing of innocent individuals because of their religion, race, or sexual preference.

From Channel Level, we are able to perceive what could be the larger lesson or plan that's unfolding through the actions of a group, an organization, a religion, or a culture. We can see patterns in the behavior of groups that lead us up the spiral of evolution—which are always due to actions taken by individuals. We all have the same purpose: to bring divine qualities into visible manifestation. As individuals, we are not generally in a position to undo global wrongs. Nevertheless, our forgiving *does* make a difference; it is the one thing that won't add to the negative frequencies that are already expressing.

In the example of being betrayed by our partner, we have now reached the understanding that every apparent wrong is ultimately not only for our good, but for that of the whole race, gender, culture, and so forth. When a critical mass of many individuals with the same perceptions has been reached, then the collective consciousness changes, seemingly overnight.

As we have taken ourselves through all of these levels of forgiveness, not only have we healed the story of being a victim, and potentially healed the ancestral patterns coming from our lineage; we have also incrementally gained greater insights and realizations into the nature of the Universe, and an expanded vision of what may be unfolding. Forgiveness has become a tool for our enlightenment. So many layers and dimensions of forgiveness have become apparent now—so many aspects of our journey that influence the world at large. Before today, we never suspected how awesome forgiveness could become.

From Oneness Level, this realization leads to the recognition that the Life of God is the only Reality, and that the belief in duality has created the materialized concepts we see: mountains, seas, creatures, everything visible. As soon as we sense the perfection of original creation, in consciousness we become One with God again. We don't need to forgive individuals for cheating, but instead recognize the perfection of the original expression of God in them, and forgive their belief that they are separate and have to seek fulfillment outside of themselves. We also forgive our own belief in duality. Then we rest in a state of forgiveness, never blaming anyone or anything.

To continually embody that state, we need to create regular habits of prayer and meditation; connect with like-minded people; get spiritual support in line with our convictions; and study inspirational material. It may be necessary to break away from a group we were with that is no longer congruent with our new perceptions.

Forgiveness no longer applies as the concept we held before. We start seeing as God sees, since the veil of separation is gone. What God sees is eternal and unchanging. If God saw evil, it would become eternal and couldn't be changed; but we know for a fact that things in this world always change, so what now seems bad can ultimately be seen as a blessing. God sees only infinite and eternal good. In Oneness consciousness, our perception becomes God's perception.

We come to the realization that forgiveness is not needed for any person or circumstance. When we forgive ourselves for the false belief in separation—which is the origin of all our problems—then through the principle of Oneness everyone else is also forgiven. There is nothing left to forgive in the physical world. Self-forgiveness of the false belief erases the misdeed. That is profound.

We need to forgive because we have been given free will to do as we choose, and we chose to act counter to the divine Law of absolute Love. God is everywhere. God is Love—not forgiveness—because "God's eyes are too pure to behold wrongdoing" (see Habakkuk 1:13).

The call for God to come into our experience must come from spiritual beings who are embodied in our three-dimensional world: free-will beings. That's you and me. God does not come to make things right, according to our human perspective. From God's perspective, everything simply is. As humans, we can't make things right; *we must see them rightly.*

HISTORICAL FORGIVENESS

At its root, harm to groups is always done by an individual—i.e., Adolf Hitler, Benito Mussolini, Idi Amin, Pol Pot, Saddam Hussein, and so on—by someone who works evil through many other individuals. An entity—like a race, religion, government, country, or organization—if we disassociate it from the individuals making it up, cannot be held responsible for the way the individuals in it are acting, even if there is a karmic imprint attached to that race or nation because of the number of people in that group holding the same mindset and expression in words and actions. Ultimately, it boils down to holding accountable the individuals in that group who have acted in damaging ways, brainwashed by their leaders who filled their minds with false and destructive ideas. We need to forgive both the individuals and the group.

When there is conflict between countries, we need to forgive the leaders and other parties. We don't hold the entire population responsible—although it's probably wise to be prudent and circumspect about interacting until we personally get to know them. It's important to have discernment.

Terrorism is undertaken by individuals indoctrinated by a group. In order to forgive, we must see the bigger picture. But that doesn't mean allowing terrorism, if we can prevent it. Even if it seems difficult to forgive war, battles, and terrorist attacks, this is where we must rise into the perspective of Source, which loves every being and everything unconditionally. Our soul is part of that Source, seeing the ultimate outcome—where every soul has established a script for itself, in agreement with every other soul involved, to move every human personality closer to the One Soul's perspective.

Whatever the conflicts or past historical events were that now need to be forgiven, everyone, in some past incarnation, wearing a different face, may have been involved in the atrocities. This is why self-forgiveness is so necessary—for things known and unknown, for all our ancestors and lineage—because ultimately, we are all one.

CULTURAL FORGIVENESS

When a certain culture rejects another culture different from its own, and this culture starts committing crimes against the people from the other culture, we can be of assistance energetically, by asking for forgiveness in the name of the culture committing the crimes. We had an example of this in 2017, during Pope Francis' visit at the refugee camp in Bangladesh, where some 650,000 members of the Rohingya tribe fled from persecutions perpetrated in Burma. This, in essence, is what the Pope said: "The presence of God, today, is also named Rohingya. In the name of all those who have persecuted you and wounded you, and also for the indifference of the world, I entreat your forgiveness. I call on your magnanimous hearts to grant us the forgiveness we implore."

In the same way, we ought to ask for forgiveness in the name of the group that is committing acts of violence and abuse. In Oneness, we are united with the perpetrators as well as with the victims. It's helpful to use the ancient Hawaiian Ho'oponopono prayer, which is so simple, and so powerful. It says that when faced with an abominable situation, whatever it is that you feel within yourself, you need to forgive, because you are totally responsible for what appears in your life. Below is an Exercise to help you do just that.

Exercise: Ho'oponopono Prayer

Address these four sentiments below to your inner child, and then to your divine aspect. You are petitioning the Divine, saying the sentences, while holding the consciousness given after each phrase.

To the inner child, the subconscious:

I love you! (Please allow me to hug you and hold you lovingly! I love you for being a part of me!)

I'm sorry! (Please help me to let go of all the memories replaying within me as limitation and doubt of any kind! I don't even know what some of those memories are, and I don't want to know; but you know; and then we can offer them to Divinity—the Superconscious—to erase. We ask Divinity to set us free!)

Please forgive me! (I have not given you recognition. You're a part of me that I have not paid much attention to. I am sorry for all the accumulated memories you experience as woe, pain, and suffering.)

Thank you! (Please give me your hand, let me stroke it gently. Thank you for being a part of me!)

To the Divine, the Superconscious:
I love you! (I am reconnecting to the Divine, which is all Love.)
I'm sorry! (I've been unconscious. I don't know where this programming came from.)
Please forgive me! (I have not been aware of the event, my actions, or my thoughts, which have created the experience I am now having.)
Thank you! (Thank you for listening to me, thank you for cleaning and clearing this, thank you for healing this within me.)

NATIONAL FORGIVENESS

There are countless examples of nations that have to be forgiven for invasions and wars, too numerous to count. Of course, every war has generated ill will and resentment, and eventually it leads to another war. If we are to stop the cycle of violence, somebody must forgive—and keep forgiving even if the aggressor assaults again. Just like where individuals are concerned, forgiving does not mean you don't defend yourself, don't stand up for what is right, or become a doormat. Forgiveness comes from the level of the consciousness from which you take the appropriate action. In the case of countries, it is more difficult to attain a collective consciousness of forgiveness while standing for justice, than it is when just a few personalities are involved.

In a country like the United States—where there are many ethnic differences such as Native Americans, African Americans, and immigrants from Europe—or in many African countries—where there are many tribes within one country—it's never an easy cut-and-dried process. Americans need to forgive each other. In Nigeria, for instance, Igbos need to forgive Hausas or Yorubas, and vice versa. The same principle applies to Nazis and Jews; to Germans and Jews; to Christians and Jews; to the Chinese and Tibetans; and on and on the list goes. We are moving forward, even if it's sometimes two steps forward and one step back.

Although we wish progress were quicker, it is the individual consciousness of each and every one of us that makes the difference. As more people stop worrying about what anyone else thinks or does, and choose to do what they know is right, there will eventually be a critical mass of people with an expanded consciousness. Then, everything will shift in the twinkling of an eye—even if there may still be pockets of dissent.

RELIGIOUS FORGIVENESS

It is important to forgive the Catholic Church for misusing power, to forgive the individuals responsible for abuses—whether mental, emotional, or physical. So much forgiveness is required for all of the ways religions have done harm because of laws and dogma wielded for personal aggrandizement, and their hurtful messages circulated, such as telling people that they will burn in hell if they disobey. Members of a religion are usually obedient, following the traditional rules—until they learn to think for themselves.

As Creators, we realize the personal responsibility we possess to decide what's right and what's wrong. We can't hide behind a law to justify an action we know to be wrong. We need to forgive both the leaders and the individuals adhering to a particular religion, who have misunderstood or misconstrued its tenets. Part of the forgiveness process here is to realize that religion itself is not responsible for a person's misunderstanding of its concepts and ideals. Most often it is institutions and leaders who manipulate and confuse.

Atrocities done in the name of religion have occurred throughout history. We only have to look at the Crusades—war after war mounted by the Catholic Church to recover the Holy Land from Muslim rule—which started in the 11th century and lasted for centuries. Then in the late 15th century there was the Spanish Inquisition, established to combat heresy and any kind of religious dissent, also lasting for hundreds of years, all the way till the early 19th century.

It really isn't any better in modern times, where ISIS in the Middle East is overrunning villages that don't have the same religious beliefs—systematically torturing and killing the men, and abusing and brutalizing the women and girls, taking them as slaves. In 2016, a girl named Ekhlas Bajoo escaped from ISIS captivity and testified in the British House of Commons about what she had witnessed. She explained that the reason the girls were being abused and brutalized was because they were Yazidis, a very ancient religious sect that believes in angels in a way that's foreign to Islam. It was because of those beliefs that they were enslaved and killed by a fundamentalist group of Muslims who were taught to fear, hate, and exterminate anyone who doesn't agree with their own beliefs.

Originally, religions were formed around certain Masters or Avatars in small villages. As people from other areas came to learn and took the wisdom back to their tribes, the original religion would change over time because of local material needs. Wars started, each religion thinking it held the only truth. Nowadays, we are witnessing some attempts at reconciliation between some religions, and some public apologies. In every religion, if we peel away the dogma and everything pertaining to physicality, what remains is the never-changing, spiritual Truth.

What if all we had to do to be in alignment with God was to forgive ourselves daily, for believing in a disconnect from Him? Then we would just need to live our normal life the best we know how. As the highest consciousness on this planet, we then become the open space through which Source can operate, in our dimension of free will. Letting Source energy express as us, everything in the world will be uplifted to its highest potential, and we can take a quantum leap into our next stage of evolution.

Let's recognize Oneness with God as our first and foremost fundamental belief—and then let's trust that this shift in our consciousness can occur. This will dissolve all other false beliefs that stem from the original error of separation. It's not even logical to believe in a severance from Spirit, when we know that Spirit is breathing us and making every organ and nerve in our body work, even without our conscious participation.

Now it is up to us to allow for continual change, as our smaller false beliefs fall away. Let us activate compassion whenever we fail to live in alignment—compassion for others, who don't even begin to understand the necessity for it; and compassion for ourselves whenever we fail to measure up. Then our ongoing work is to develop spiritual sight, seeing in every challenge the possibility of having a higher response than a habitual material one.

We don't need to know how to forgive, when to forgive, what to forgive, or why to forgive—we simply forgive with every breath. This is how we'll bring Divinity into this world, transformed by forgiveness. Over time, the world will start reflecting the Light we have become.

GENDER FORGIVENESS

Gender supremacy between men and women has been alternating in cycles of approximately 12,000 years. We hear of it in such legends as the Amazons, where women held all the power and men were relegated to tasks that demanded only physical strength; this structure was not allowing the men to evolve. The men became protectors of the women, slowly gained power, and then started repressing them. This was enabling the progress of each gender in turn. We have now just come into a new cycle, where women are being empowered again. Finding a way to have equal power without repressing the other gender is the task facing us now, so that we can all progress together.

If you're a woman, most likely you need to forgive men in general. And men need to forgive the feminine, or women in general. That's a deep-seated wound inside all of us. Women need to forgive the masculine for abuses, and forgive themselves for how they have given up their power. Perhaps we can even forgive the feminine that has failed to stand in its power, blaming the masculine. Men also need to forgive themselves and the masculine for the way they so often come from a wounded place to hurt women.

ORGANIZATIONS AND INDUSTRIES

Industrial corporations often pervert the laws of nature, damaging whole populations for the profit of the few. Again, it's the top layer of individuals that is really responsible. We must find a way to forgive their mindset by elevating our consciousness into the spiritual realm, while counteracting their activities.

For example, the food industry uses pesticides harmful to our health, which throw the whole ecosystem out of balance. They destroy bugs, insects, bees, and other lifeforms essential for the good functioning of the planet as a whole. Now apples look appetizing, without blemishes, but their content in vitamins has gone down so much that we have to take supplements—which we buy from the pharmaceutical industry.

There are so many genetically altered plants, that there is an increasing risk of disrupting our whole economy, because their seeds can no longer germinate. Pharmaceutical industries create drugs with secondary effects that necessitate the use of more drugs, when we actually have homeopathic medicines and plenty of alternative healing modalities that use no drugs at all. Not to mention experimentation on animals, which still exists, showing our total lack of respect for divine creation. A lot needs to change in these areas; and we are just starting to see some of these unsustainable practices being denounced and abolished. Now that this forgiveness process has begun, with our diligence, it will continue.

CHAPTER 12

CONCLUSION—FORGIVENESS AS A WAY OF LIFE

Forgiveness is about empowering yourself, rather than empowering your past.
—T. D. Jakes

FORGIVENESS AS A LIFELONG PATH

If we look at the structure of forgiveness, we see that there are steps that gradually allow us to reach higher levels. This is called the Ascension Path.

We first identify where a hurt has been caused; identify what it's really about; identify the lesson or the blessing; learn and grow from it; and then let go of whatever is left over. Then we have to stand up for what we need, while wishing only the best for the perpetrator. We forgive everything daily, just like we take a bath or shower every day to clean accumulated dirt—in this case, we forgive again in order to eliminate any lingering animosity. That's the way to live life every day; when it's embodied, we don't hold onto things. We respond to what happens through this integrated forgiveness framework.

Taking again the example of betrayal I have been using, we acknowledge we were hurt, but then focus back on ourselves: The person who needs attention, love, and nurturing is us. We give to ourselves what our partner could not give us by recognizing our true nature, which is divine.

You are the one and only Source, having aspects of Truth, Love, Joy, Harmony, Happiness, Peace, and so on—choose whatever name resonates for you. You as Source, send aspects of Yourself we call *souls* into the world, carrying more of the quality each name represents. Now imagine you are the aspect of Divinity called *Forgiveness*, and your birth name—say, *Susan*—is the name of the experience of being in a body. So you, Susan the body, are a unique experience of the divine aspect called Forgiveness, and you are experiencing the relationship other bodies have with the Divinity of their true nature. Susan is the experience, not the Experiencer. You realize that the transgression or abuse wasn't against you, it was just demonstrating your partner's less-than-conscious relationship with his or her own Divinity. Now, forgiveness is needed first and foremost for you—Susan, the experience—for thinking that you were the subject of anyone's offensive behavior; because really, you were only experiencing in your body your partner's relationship with the Divine. When you experience anything you don't like, you might become aware that others may have no time for you, and perhaps they have no interest in your well-being; it is now up to you to provide for yourself what only your Divinity can ever provide.

Forgiving another person is wonderful, but it doesn't really get you to evolve fully. What does get you to a higher level—where forgiveness is not even part of your vocabulary—is realizing your true divine nature, which can never be harmed in any way. This whole book is about evolving yourself out of the need to forgive, even if that enlightenment may never come in this lifetime. No sincere effort is ever lost. Every attempt moves us closer to our goal.

CONCLUSION—FORGIVENESS AS A WAY OF LIFE

When we discover the real meaning of the event, we see that it was an expression of what our partner needed and wanted; it was not directed against us personally. Our partner's actions brought into visibility what was hidden inside us—sadness, resentment, confusion, fear, victimhood, or *good riddance*! The purpose was to make us aware of the feelings that were hiding, which needed to be brought to the surface so that they could be released. It may not have been possible, or safe, to express those feelings openly before; now from the perspective of an adult, it's time to let go of anything that no longer serves us. Maybe we weren't able to discern our partner's needs. Perhaps we were not aware enough, so part of the responsibility for the event is ours. The experience has been useful and beneficial, since we learned something and became more conscious.

We harvest the lessons and blessings of the event. If it was very traumatic, we may need some time. We may only see the blessings in retrospect—five or ten years later. When we know ourselves— know our needs and motivations, and know who we are, nothing can be a threat.

Our quality of life can only improve if we start asking better questions. The mentality of *Why is this happening to me? I don't deserve this!* is the Victim mentality, where we're not yet realizing that the power to change our life lies within us. We must claim this power, and exercise it. Thus our new questions are *What's the lesson in this experience? How is it benefitting me? How will I grow because of this? What qualities has it already activated?* We start to realize *I am more resilient, I am more tough-minded, I can handle more! I have become more resourceful!* If we are doing this throughout our days, there is nothing left to be forgiven. It becomes the way we process life.

When we ask *Now that I've lost my relationship, what is the principle of life I need to discover?* The answer comes: the principle that Life is One—that Life is Joy, Love, Harmony, and Abundance. So, when I seem to lose materially, the truth is, I can never be alone—and I will never lack supply, friendship, love, or peace—because I am one with the infinite Source of All. Wanting the best for the offender is the next step—without resentment or blame, and even with a measure of gratitude.

Blaming someone or something for how we feel is unproductive, keeping us in Victim consciousness. Remember, our feelings are just *e-motions*—energies that move through us as we observe and acknowledge them. True forgiveness starts with *I feel sad and hurt, but I don't know why*. After we become clear—completely honest and open about what we feel and need, and receptive to what our partner feels and needs—we must unequivocally stand for that. Our partner's needs never overshadow our own; we are equals. A relationship that really works is always 200 percent—an investment of 100 percent from each person. It's never about taking turns, or based on paybacks. While you give without reservation, be open to receiving, and be grateful that your partner knows what your needs are, through the deep, meaningful conversations you have about life. There will then be continual transformation for both of you, because life is never static and never over.

This whole journey of forgiveness is really much more than just forgiving; it's about illuminating our path. This work can be applied to any quality we think is lacking, or to any characteristic we want to enhance. For instance, when we look at *trust, safety, security, love, peace,* or *harmony*, at what stage of consciousness are we when we consider those attributes in our own lives? Going deeply into any quality, we can discover the same journey—from the unconscious to the fully conscious. This process is a universal framework which, in this book, I have applied to forgiveness. What does love, peace, or harmony look like when you are in Victim, Creator, or Channel consciousness?

Exercise: How to see our Oneness with another

This exercise can be applied when you need to forgive, or as training for seeing the underlying Oneness—of you and another person of your choice.

Take a few deep breaths and get to a place of stillness and peace. Close your eyes, and put yourself and the other person on the screen of your mind.

Now in your mind's eye, see yourself standing on the left and notice what you look like, what you're wearing, your hair, your expression, mannerisms, and behavior. Now look beyond the appearance level, and see the Light in your heart shining brightly. As you're looking at that Light, it begins to expand and radiate throughout your body and spreads outside, forming a shimmering oval of Light around you.

Now turn your mind's eye to the right, and see the other person standing there, and again notice what that person looks like—clothes, characteristics, and movements. Now expand your perception beyond what the physical appearance is, to the Light within this individual's heart. And as you look at it, it intensifies and spreads until it fills up the inside of the body, and then extends beyond the body, and keeps expanding.

Now, look at the space that was between the two of you, and see the Light from both hearts, expanding to meet each other. Now there is no more space in between. As you witness the intensification of the Light, the bodies seem to grow fainter, dissolving into a shadow and then

> gradually disappearing, until all that's left is the Light—in which you two are One.
>
> Simply see it—witness it, and know it, and realize that forgiveness is no longer needed. The only Reality is that Light. The body is an illusion. Be still—and know that the Light that is your Oneness together is real. Spend a few moments breathing deeply—just breathing in that Reality.

We will have to continue forgiving as long as we see any wrong. It's through doing forgiveness work that perceptions change. As long as there is pain, help is needed from our true nature. We ask sincerely: *God, help me to forgive, give me the insights that will make me see the Truth—that no harm has ever been done!*

In the case of betrayal, maybe what you finally understand is that you have put together two separate events—the fact that your partner sought consolation with someone else, and the fact that you were feeling abandoned—with a conclusion that *that* was a betrayal. Instead, you could decide that events don't cause each other—they just happen—and no one is to be blamed for anything. Life, mercifully, provides you with a ready-made reason so that your mind stops searching. You can now even become grateful for that apparent reason. *Thank you, Life! And thank you, my partner! I am grateful that you've made it possible for me to sit with all these feelings, be with them, and see and hear them, so that they can finally be transmuted.*

CONCLUSION—FORGIVENESS AS A WAY OF LIFE

THE "FORGIVEN LIFE" VISION PROCESS

You have gone through this book, deeply considered and possibly healed those aspects that felt sad, rejected, or unforgiving. You can see different priorities needing to take precedence over those you had in the past; you can tell how much of your reaction to a problem is coming from past wounds, and how much is coming from the present incident. If you've really forgiven yourself and everyone else, basically you are living a life where nothing is a problem.

In a truly forgiven life, you have the ability to deal with things as they arise, with what's really going on. Only rarely is what's arising all that bad—that is, when you are not unknowingly bringing the past into it. As a result, your consciousness will be such that it's no longer defending, fighting, protecting, or trying to prove anything. The signal that you're going to be radiating out to others is one of safety, security, love, and abundance; this practice will manifest more and more of those qualities to you, instead of the previous lack and limitation.

Whenever the ego perceives a hurt or wrong of any kind, you resolve the war between your true divine nature and your personality—by forgiving instead of by lashing out and blaming. You become your true nature, and radiate *that* to any people who touch your field of experience, so that they are inspired to express more of *their* true nature. Can you see how, just by changing yourself, you are also changing the world around you?

Now you know how to create the life you really want—a life that you live on purpose, the way you want it to be. You have a much clearer idea of the vision for your life. You need to put certain practices in place, so that you don't just react to circumstances, getting pulled this way and that by the outside world. Some of these new habits might include making time for prayer and meditation, for fun activities with your family, and for exercising on a regular basis.

You now live in a state of allowance and love—and that is forgiveness! There is not a single person or situation you can think of that doesn't bring a smile to your face—or at the very least, you're neutral. You have taken your life into your own hands, knowing you are sovereign. This will make you a strong anchor for your family—a responsible person in your job and in your life. You're not waiting for anyone's validation or approval.

Take some time just to imagine and envision your life as you're living it day by day, and how it might look when you have totally forgiven everyone for everything—including yourself.

When you see a white-haired couple on a park bench squabbling, the only thought that arises is *Aren't they sweet? Just like two little kids!*

When you see real anger between people, you feel compassion, knowing they must be in great pain.

You've missed your bus going to work? Instead of being angry and upset, you realize there will be another one soon. You use the time to bless the people in the cars that pass by.

In your professional life, you are radiating love and appreciation—not even noticing that your boss seems not to like you, or that colleagues don't support you—because you know your own worth. You are always considerate and thoughtful when listening to problems and difficulties. Pretty soon, you'll find yourself loved and appreciated, or you will be harmoniously moved out of that environment to one that is congruent with the person you have become.

Your sense of knowing that you are divine always leads you to being at peace with whatever is appearing. You know that appearances change all the time; *it's the consciousness you have about them that matters.* You are grateful for the finances you have, knowing they are enough, however little they may seem at times. That trust and gratitude will free you of worry and anxiety, allowing you to show peacefulness in all situations. This spiritual practice will teach your

CONCLUSION—FORGIVENESS AS A WAY OF LIFE

family and friends that Life is always supportive, so long as they uphold themselves also.

There is no more stress in your life, so your overall health and your level of energy are better than ever before; you may not even know how or why. You walk in nature, go on trips with family and friends, and visualize what else you want to do. Maybe you want to swim with the dolphins, or climb Mount Everest! Anything can become your reality. You start feeling that whatever happens, everything will be okay. Your reality will start reflecting this new mindset. When you believe that the Universe is friendly, it will be a friend to you.

You know that your desire for something means that it's meant to be yours. And it will be—as soon as you've embodied the qualities a person living that life must have, in order not to misuse that gift.

Imagine you have totally forgiven yourself for every occurrence where you did not show up as well as you could have. Imagine being without guilt or shame. Make a commitment that from this day, you will honor and respect all people you meet—whoever they are—so each person feels seen, accepted, and valued.

Imagine your kids trusting your love, knowing that they can count on you in every circumstance. They grow up to be strong, joyful, kind, considerate individuals—transmitting your values to their families, their friends, and their communities, to many people you may never even know. And this love and esteem goes on for generation after generation, creating increasing goodwill and harmony, until there is peace on earth among all people and all nations.

The old world of separation, conflict, powerlessness, and disease has vanished, because we have ended the war between the parts of ourselves that were created by our judgment of certain painful events. Fear, doubt, and selfishness—now integrated—have become love, trust, and self-care. When we accept every negative aspect as divine—just temporarily misperceived—then we can see everyone else in that light also.

The new world will be a place where everyone is important, empowered, joyful, and happy—and isn't that vision worth every effort we make to be the best version of ourselves? There is only One Life, One Energy, One Spirit. Whatever we do from the consciousness of Oneness will influence and permeate the consciousness of all.

Imagine the highest vision you can dream up. Refine it to the point where it feels like there could not be a better life. Now, start taking small steps towards it. Synchronicities will happen, doors will open, and it will all be exciting and joyful. That's what your life could be. Imagine where you will live, and with whom—your family, your kids, and friends nearby. Make it detailed—the house, the yard, the surroundings. And then decide *What will fill my days?* What would a day in your ideal life look like, from the time you wake up to the time you go to bed? There will be time for prayer and meditation, time for family, time for the work you want to do, and so forth. Decide upon your contribution to Life—how to share your wisdom, talents, and abilities with others. Ask *What else do I want?*

Everything you have just envisioned can happen now because you have established daily spiritual practices to make forgiveness a way of life. Your new habits will continue to build the character of a confident, capable, loving, allowing, supportive, and generative being. You are clear on what you want and how to achieve it.

Anything that comes into your field of experience is automatically forgiven, because that's the frequency you carry when you no longer have judgment or resistance. When darkness meets Light, darkness is no more. Forgiveness is the process by which you remove blocks and obstacles to the full expression of your infinite and unlimited life and potential. The by-product is more life, more love, more abundance, and more creativity—simply because more of you is emerging and manifesting.

CONCLUSION—FORGIVENESS AS A WAY OF LIFE

This isn't forgiveness for forgiveness' sake. It's the liberation of your power and potential, extending to all whose lives you touch.

That's the legacy you will leave when you decide to go for your highest vision and to live life as the divine being you really are, never giving up. You are the Source and the Cause of your life.

The bigger picture of what our lives are meant to be is usually hidden, but sometimes we get insights about why things happen as they do. For me, as I've said, I woke at 3:00 a.m. one night, clearly knowing why I had read a certain book when I was nine years old, and how it sparked a desire to be able to forgive incredible personal wrongs, and how that desire was fulfilled some 60 years later. Without that moment, this book would never have been written. Even though I no longer have descendants to transmit my ideals to, maybe a faster way to bring forgiveness and peace to the world than through generations of children and grandchildren is to do it through a book which can help thousands, all at once—to implement an even higher legacy. A legacy of forgiveness.

If this was the reason for my challenges and heartbreak, it's a small price indeed to pay.

What if, at this time on our planet, when everything is changing faster than ever before, it has become a necessity for us to approach life's challenges with a different outlook—of allowance and forgiveness, without judgment? If enough of us were to awaken to this fact, then peace within each person, peace between individuals, and peace among communities and nations would happen, in every corner of the world simultaneously.

APPENDIX

ADDITIONAL EXERCISES

Releasing Balloons Exercise

(Can be used at Level 1 or 2.)

In a case where you have someone you need to forgive, and even though you've often tried, that person keeps coming into your awareness, then the individual is still energetically attached to you. Try doing this:

Write the name of the person—as well as the wrongdoing committed, if there is still a charge around that—on a strip of paper. Now, get a red balloon. Slide your strip of paper into the balloon, and then blow it up, as big as you can get it, tying up the end tight, imprisoning the name and the problem inside. The red color symbolizes a red light, a stop sign—an end to the painful feelings in your awareness.

Take the balloon out on a walk in nature or by the sea, preferably on a very windy day, and very consciously say to the person and the event inside the balloon: I forgive you. May you be peaceful, joyful, and happy. I release you from my life!

Now let go of the string, and consciously watch the balloon being blown by the wind up into the atmosphere and float away, to be lost in space.

Four Exercises to Release Core Emotions

(Can be used at Levels 1, 2, or 3.)

Anger and hurt are root emotions. They will almost always result in health issues—especially inflammation, which results from inflamed emotions. It takes time to release old hurts! These exercises will help move the process along.

Releasing Anger
When you're angry at people, realize that coupled with the anger is also a feeling of blame for what they said or did. Stop focusing on them, or on what happened, and just focus on the feeling of anger inside of you, without looking for a cause. Intensify it, and try to feel angrier still! Don't allow any thoughts of I shouldn't feel this way come in. In other words, give yourself permission to get angrier and angrier, watch yourself getting more and more angry, and within a few minutes you will realize that you can't even find the anger any more. It will even start to feel slightly ridiculous to be that angry. You will manage to laugh at yourself, and soon you'll see that you're free of it.

Releasing Hurt or Sadness

Turn on a timer for 20 minutes. In those 20 minutes feel the hurt or sadness as deeply as you can, focusing exclusively on that feeling. After 2 to 3 minutes, you will find that it's really hard to force yourself to stay hurt or sad. When the timer rings, then completely drop it. Go into a different state of mind. Look out the window. Notice something interesting. Think about a totally unrelated past or upcoming event.

Then nurture yourself. Make a plan for how you want to pamper yourself in some way. Have a hot bath, sit in the sun, read a good book, or play some music. Cherish yourself—appreciate and love yourself—for one whole hour. That's the most important step in this process!

Releasing Shame

This one you can't process like anger, sadness, or hurt. Shame was not yours to begin with. It was never true. Shame means that someone else made you feel small, deficient, less than human.

Sit in a quiet space and bring to mind the person who made you feel ashamed, and get angry at that individual. How dare you give me such a feeling? And why did I ever accept it as mine? Imagine that all of that shame goes into a paper bag you are holding, and envision walking up to the person, and giving it back.

Tell that person: This is yours! I want to give it back to you, because it never belonged to me! It's okay to return it, because you are not wanting to hurt this person. You are just releasing yourself from the emotion that's in the bag.

Releasing Guilt

Guilt is really anger, which you feel you have no right to express. It's easy to blame yourself for what you've done; but it's unproductive. You need to turn that guilt into anger, and then process the anger. (See the Exercise on Releasing Anger, above.)

If you really look for it, there is always some anger underlying guilt. If you have hurt someone, or a dog runs under your tires and you feel guilty, the anger is usually at yourself. Also explore anger in other areas of your life that you are not letting yourself feel. Process those, by fully feeling them, and intensifying them if need be, as in the Releasing Anger Exercise above.

Beyond Forgiveness Exercise

(For use in late Level 2, or Level 3.)

Look through your past, to any instances when you were upset, harmed, attacked, or devalued in some way. Maybe someone hit you, or worse; perhaps atrocities happened — and you are now looking at all of that.

When you're ready, pour unconditional love into those memory pictures. See the whole scene in your mind, see all the people involved, see what happened, and replay that event in your mind.

Now, let's stop the film. Take seven deep breaths to relax yourself, and start with a prayer: I AM of Source, I AM anchored in God, I accept this healing for my highest good. Then say the following sentence nine times — slowly, and

APPENDIX

feeling every word of it—to the person or persons involved in that event: I thank you for this participation in my journey, done for my highest good. I bless you on your journey, and I send you my unconditional love.

Feel the relaxation of knowing that everything happens only for your highest good. Finish up with a prayer: Thank You, God, thank You, Source. I send You my unconditional love. And so it is. And so I let it be.

ABOUT THE AUTHOR

Jania Aebi was not always a transformational energy healer; that's a relatively recent chapter in her life. Born in Poland before WWII, Jania knew only war and strife during her childhood and early teens. During her adult life in West Africa, she was in the midst of civil wars during the 1960s. Her life tragically changed after her husband died in a plane crash and her only child was murdered. There was no more human logic to lean on, and an impossible forgiveness to be found. She had to search deeper than ever in order to survive.

Challenges have always shaped Jania. She escaped Poland with her mother and siblings to settle in England, where she finished her education. Longing for adventure, she found a job in Nigeria with an import/export company, where she met her Swiss husband. For about thirty years, they lived in West Africa, where their only son was born. It was partly an enchanted life—visiting game parks, going on safaris, and living close to nature, even if always in capital cities. And it was also partly a difficult time, living in the midst of civil wars or ethnic disturbances in one country after another. That idyllic life came to an end when her husband died in a plane crash. She left Togo, where her husband was then stationed, to start a new life in Switzerland, a country she didn't even know.

Between the grief of losing her husband, raising their 13-year-old boy alone, and trying not to sink into despair, Jania had to discover inner resources, which didn't seem to exist outside. She began her journey on a path of spirituality, which would become her guiding force. Years later, when her son was murdered—as fate would have it, also in Africa—he died in a coma just as her husband had died. Jania had to be the one to remove her son's ventilator. At that point, something cracked open. There was no more hope, no one to live for. She knew something had radically changed.

Jania searched for the real reasons behind why things happen. She studied, read, prayed, and meditated. At one point, at the age of 75, she was gifted with the clear knowledge that she was a healer—something she knew absolutely nothing about. She committed to it instantly, with just one condition. She said aloud to God *You have to bring me everything I need, as I don't even know where to begin*. As a result, a condition in her foot, which appeared to have gangrene, and which no doctor could remedy, disappeared overnight.

In the next few years Jania's life changed again, from spiritual learning to becoming an energy healer. The modalities she needed have always been miraculously brought to her; she never had to search for anything. Her private healing practice organically developed into a business—something she never even sought after. Nevertheless, it led to her writing her first book, *Your Infinite Power*; then to a radio show; and on to a coaching career. It seems that her life has been one continuous stream of doing things she knows absolutely nothing about.

Jania's commitment is to heal, awaken, and transform all beings, to create a world where people respect, value, and appreciate each other and all of creation—a world that works for the highest good of all. Unconditionally forgiving everyone for everything, including ourselves, is entirely necessary if we are to create that world.

It is her hope that *Forgiveness—A Path to Create Miracles* will help many to find happiness for themselves, and that her readers will also share the book with others.

ACKNOWLEDGMENTS

My deepest love and gratitude goes to so many, it's impossible to enumerate them all; but I especially want to express it, first and foremost, to my own Higher Self, which guided me unerringly to the people and the resources I needed to find my mission in this lifetime and gave me the courage to pursue it. My profound thanks also to:

My son Albert, who gave his own life for my growth and evolution, and to M. F., who unknowingly fulfilled his part in the contract the three of us had made and forgotten.

Derek Rydall, my mentor and teacher, who believed in me when I did not, encouraged and supported me when I was close to quitting, and held space for me that allowed me to grow. Without him, this book would not have been written.

Ken Stone, for his witnessing me and facilitating experiences that can't be put into words.

Elizabeth Mallet, for her unconditional acceptance of me as I am.

Thomas and Marys Potocki for their support in the hard times and for their unfailing love, friendship, and understanding.

The Michel family—Nancy, Philippe, Marc, Anna and Christel—who provide kindness, love, fun and games, tech knowledge, and boundless support.

BIBLIOGRAPHY

Archer, Marlo. "Maybe So, Maybe Not. We'll See." Down to Earth Enterprises. www.drmarlo.com/?page_id=181. [Zen proverb].

BBC News. "Spain Women: Top Court Rules Wolf Pack Gang Were Rapists." www.bbc.com/news/world-europe-48716940. [Spain rape case].

Berlinger, Joshua and Delia Gallagher. "Pope Francis: 'The Presence of God Today Is also Called Rohingya.'" CNN World, December 1, 2017. www.cnn.com/2017/12/01/asia/pope-bangladesh-myanmar-intl. [Pope Francis visiting Bangladesh in 2017 after the Rohingya genocide].

Berry, Jack W. and Everett L. Worthington Jr. "Forgivingness, Relationship Quality, Stress while Imagining Relationship Events, and Physical and Mental Health." Journal of Counseling Psychology 48(4): 447–455. 2001. DOI 10.1037/0022-0167.48.4.447.

Bolte, Jill. My Stroke of Insight: A Brain Scientist's Personal Journey. London: Penguin, 2009. [About holding a thought for 90 seconds].

Chida, Y. and A. Steptoe. "Positive Psychological Well-Being and Mortality: A Quantitative Review of Prospective Observational Studies." Psychosomatic Medicine, Aug 25, 2008, Sep;70(7):741-56. DOI 10.1097/PSY.0b013e31818105ba.

Dalai Lama. Spirituality Quotation. https://www.spiritualityandpractice.com/quotes/quotations/view/24523/spiritual-quotation. [Tibetan monk story].

Hodal, Kate. "Impunity Reigns: Six Survivors of Sexual Violence Speak Out." The Guardian, 2019. https://www.theguardian.com/global-development/2019/jun/24/impunity-reigns-six-survivors-of-sexual-violence-speak-out. [Ekhlas Bajoo story].

Holt-Lunstad, Julianne, Timothy W. Smith, Bert N. Uchino. "Can Hostility Interfere with the Health Benefits of Giving and Receiving Social Support? The Impact of Cynical Hostility on Cardiovascular Reactivity during Social Support Interactions among Friends." Annals of Behavioral Medicine, June 27, 2008, 35:319–330. DOI 10.1007/s12160-008-9041-z.

Hu, J. and K. J. Gruber. "Positive and Negative Affect and Health Functioning Indicators among Older Adults with Chronic Illnesses." Issues in Mental Health Nursing, August 29, 2008, Aug;29(8):895–911. DOI 10.1080/01612840802182938.

Kahn, Matt. "Seven Holy Words." www.youtube.com/watch?v=50UYrn0iQrs. [Achieving Oneness in chapter 10].

Kor, Eva Mozes. "I survived the Holocaust Twin Experiments.". https://www.youtube.com/watch?v=gdgPAetNY5U&inf_contact_key=f7523d34f86d0d14d0bb7e3e07d3be72. 2017 [Story of a Holocaust survivor].

Kornfield, Jack. "The Ancient Heart of Forgiveness." Greater Good Magazine, August 23, 2011. https://greatergood.berkeley.edu/article/item/the_ancient_heart_of_forgiveness. [Young murderer's story].

Lawler, Kathleen A., Jarred W. Younger, Rachel L. Piferi et al. "The Unique Effects of Forgiveness on Health: An Exploration of Pathways." Journal of Behavioral Medicine, 28, 157–167 (2005). DOI 10.1007/s10865-005-3665-2.

McCullough, Michael E. Beyond Revenge: The Evolution of the Forgiveness Instinct. San Francisco: Jossey-Bass, 2008.

McCullough, Michael E. "Forgiveness: Who Does It and How Do They Do It?" Current Directions in Psychological Science, December 10, 2001, Vol. 10, Number 6, 194–197, 1111/1467-8721.00147.

Pradervand, Pierre. "A Stunning Lesson on Forgiveness." The Gentle Art of Blessing. https://gentleartofblessing.org/a-stunning-lesson-on-forgiveness. [Story in chapter 11].

Ramani, Donato. "The Neuroanatomical Basis for Forgiveness Revealed." NeuroscienceNews.com, April 10, 2017. https://neurosciencenews.com/forgiveness-neurobiology-6373. Source: SISSA research project published in Scientific Reports, April 6, 2017, DOI 10.1038/srep45967, https://www.nature.com/articles/srep45967.

Reed, Gayle L. and Robert D. Enright. "The Effects of Forgiveness Therapy on Depression, Anxiety, and Posttraumatic Stress for Women after Spousal Emotional Abuse." Journal of Consulting and Clinical Psychology, October 2006, 74(5), 920–929. DOI 10.1037/0022-006X.74.5.920.

Sandoiu, Ana. "Why Do Some of Us Find it Easier to Forgive? Neuroscience Sheds Light." Medical News Today, April 16, 2017. https://www.medicalnewstoday.com/articles/316901.php#1.

Serenity Prayer. AA History. [Forgiving others, chapter 8]. http://www.aahistory.com/prayer.html#:~:targetText=%22God%20grant%20us%20the%20serenity,contained%20in%20the%20prayer's%20thoughts.

Stoia-Caraballo, Rebecca, Mark S. Rye, Wei Pan, Keri J. Brown Kirschman, Catherine Lutz-Zois, and Amy M. Lyons. "Negative Affect and Anger Rumination as Mediators between Forgiveness and Sleep Quality." Journal of Behavioral Medicine, October 2008, 31(6), 478–488. DOI 10.1007/s10865-008-9172-5.

Toussaint, Loren L., Everett L. Worthington Jr., and David R. Williams. Forgiveness and Health: Scientific Evidence and Theories Relating Forgiveness to Better Health. New York: Springer, 2015.

Vitale, Joe, Ihaleakala Len Hew. Zero Limits: The Secret Hawaiian System for Wealth, Health, Peace, and More. Hoboken, New Jersey: John Wiley & Sons, 1953. [Ho'oponopono exercise in chapter 11].

West, Matthew. "Forgiveness Is Like the Weather." FaithGateway, October 17, 2014. https://www.faithgateway.com/forgiveness-is-like-the-weather/#.XF156NFCdTJ. [Alice's story of forgiveness].

Worthington, Everett L. Jr., Charlotte Van Oyen Witvliet, Pietro Pietrini, and Andrea. J. Miller. "Forgiveness, Health, and Well-Being: A Review of Evidence for Emotional versus Decisional Forgiveness, Dispositional Forgivingness, and Reduced Unforgiveness." Journal of Behavioral Medicine, April 24, 2007, 30:291–302. DOI 10.1007/s10865-007-9105-8. https://www.ncbi.nlm.nih.gov/pubmed/?term=Worthington%2CWitvliet%2C++Pietrini%2C.

Worthington, Everett L. Jr. "The New Science of Forgiveness." Greater Good Magazine, September 1, 2004. https://greatergood.berkeley.edu/article/item/the_new_science_of_forgiveness. [Chris Carrier story].

www.ingramcontent.com/pod-product-compliance
Lightning Source LLC
Chambersburg PA
CBHW072002110526
44592CB00012B/1178